Day Trading for a Living
for Noobs

*Everything You Need to Know to Start Day
Trading for a Living*

By

Laurence Price

COPYRIGHT

FOR NOOBS BOOKS

Books for Noobs make discovering new skills quickly and easily. Open the door to your potential.

Today, in a busy world dominated by technology and increasingly busy schedules, it's challenging to find time to read and gain new skills. Books can be overwhelming. Many people want to read but are not able to.

As authors and publishers, we want our audience to learn any potentially complex topic they desire. So, we focused our efforts on creating books that do just that.

Books for Noobs. Short, straight to the point, easy, and fun books to read.

Readers at any level can engage with and learn many different topics. With a commitment to creating and maintaining the highest standards, Books for Noobs makes learning about things easier. Readers will finally be able to discover new subjects and make time to finish books.

Books for Noobs are great reads for anyone looking for ideas, inspiration, wisdom and encouragement. They also make great gifts.

www.booksfornoobs.com

YOUR FREE GIFT

Thanks for buying my book!

To show my appreciation, I would like to invite you to the For Noobs Book Club and send you a FREE BONUS BOOK: ***Stock Investing for Noobs – The Easiest Step-by-Step Investment Guide with Zero-Knowledge Prerequisite***

The perfect starting place to better understand stock investments in a simple and easy to understand language.

The book will cover:

- **"Finding the Right Industries to Invest In"** (finding industries that interest you, but also those that will be able to sail through economic storms).

- **"The Important Rules of Investing"** (approved tips to help you make the best use of your money).

- **"How to Value Stocks"** (Calculated predictions of how well a stock will do in the long and short term).

- **"Growth Investing Strategies"** (growth investing strategy focuses on businesses that have excellent growth value).

- And Much More!

Download your FREE copy today, visit the link below and sign up now:

>>>bit.ly/noobinvesting<<<

DISCLAIMER

The author and the company (www.booksfornoobs.com), including anyone involved or affiliated with the company, are NOT an investment advisory service. This book is not intended to advise on what securities readers should buy to sell for themselves. There is a high degree of risk involved in trading securities, and this must be understood. And while this book suggests careful understanding and research before investing, the company, author, and affiliates of the company assume no liability or responsibility for investment and trading results. These statements made as of the date stated are subject to change without notice. The methods, indicators, or techniques should not be assumed to result in profits or losses. All processes, indicators, techniques, strategies, and rules in this book are provided for informational and educational purposes only and not created as investment advice. Examples and stories are presented for educational purposes only. Hence, a reader should not solely rely on the information in this book to make trades or investments. Instead, they should only use the information in this book as a starting point to inspire more independent research to allow the formation of their own opinions regarding trading and investments. Investors and traders need to confer with their licensed financial advisors and tax advisors to identify any suitable investment.

TABLE OF CONTENTS

INTRODUCTION – MY STORY

There's a saying that goes something like this, "you're driven to seek success through either inspiration or desperation." I wish I could say that I was ONLY inspired to become a day trader, but my story is a bit of both. I'm grateful, though. Otherwise, I would still be stuck in an unfulfilling career, feeling that I wasn't living to my potential. There had to be more to my career and life.

I was like many people in this world. I wanted a different life. Have you ever sat for hours and hours watching paint dry? That's what my job felt like. It was so dull. I was doing the same thing day in and day out, not even having to think. Just mindlessly doing my work on autopilot, doing enough to keep my job. Don't get me wrong. There's nothing wrong with working a traditional job. But, I felt like I was meant for more. Living a safe and simple life felt almost depressing at times. However, I needed the paycheck to pay my rent and buy groceries every month. Despite all that, I had dreams and goals and fantasized about them becoming a reality through chance. Even though I wasn't happy with my ordinary life, I didn't look for another one, and I made no real effort to change things. I figured that was it for me… A mediocre life where I built a little nest egg to sustain me and blended into the crowd in this endless rat race.

Then I was rudely thrown out of my comfort zone. Actually, it felt more like being drop-kicked out, WWE-style. I lost my job and suddenly the security I thought I had in my career was gone, just like that. Poof! The whole industry I was working in was tanking, too, so getting another job doing what I already knew how to do anywhere close to where I lived was almost impossible, even though I had a university degree and job experience. Cue the sad, hopeless music; that was how I felt at the time—hopeless.

Call it what you will—God, luck, or plain old coincidence—that I ran into a friend while mindlessly walking around, trying to figure out the next step in my life. Seriously, you could have taken me straight off the set of the making of *Bittersweet Symphony* by The Verve—hands in my pockets, dismal look on my face, the whole thing. You'll get the picture if you see the music video.

We literally walked straight into each other, or rather, I walked right into him since I was deep in thought and not paying attention to where I was going. After mumbling, "Sorry," I was going to continue along my way, but then I heard the man say my name like a question, like he thought he recognized me but wasn't sure.

"Laurence?"

I looked up quickly, snapped back to the present, and squinted as I tried to place the face.

"Jeff?" I said a moment later, and then the two of us were doing that back-slapping hug that men always seem to do.

Jeff and I had gone to elementary school and high school together and had been best friends for almost ten years before moving to another state. We had lost touch, but that was one of the most treasured friendships of my life.

Jeff invited me for a coffee, and I took him up on his offer. We got talking, and at the risk of sounding obsessed, I told the man how radiant he looked! He seemed so happy that he glowed while I was eating a massive bowl of depression pie since I lost my job.

Jeff just laughed at my awkward compliment. He told me what he'd been doing for work. Day trading. And it had been nearly ten years since starting it. He wasn't shy about telling me his accomplishments with this career and how happy he was about the success. The crazy part was that I had known Jeff since we were kids, and back then, he had always talked about his dream to become a veterinarian. A career in finance was the last thing I imagined this guy would end up in.

"Anyone can become a day trader."

That had been his reply as he shrugged like that was obvious.

After, my mind was whirling and refused to rest. "Anyone can do it," Jeff had said, and I thought, "so why can't I?"

As soon as I got home, I started up my laptop and began to research. My mind gobbled up one blog post, then another, article after article, one report after another as I browsed the Internet. I spent the entire night on the computer, totally hooked on learning about day trading and financial markets. The logical part of my brain was fascinated by the challenges described in such a career. I felt a fire inside me that hadn't been ignited in a very long time.

There certainly had not been any fire inspired by my previous job. That feeling led me to realize that I needed to overhaul my life and make moves that would make me feel proud of myself. I had just been existing—a drone doing the same things over and over without a thought. It was time to start living, and my career was where I needed to make that change.

My search led me to plenty of books on the topic of day trading, as well as a ton of videos and podcasts. I had heard of day trading before, but I never thought about doing it for a living. I always imagined it as a career where you'd be living in New York and working on Wall

Street, having fancy qualifications and a particular personality type.

How had I been wrong about all those things? I discovered that I could work from the comfort of my own home and make more money than I ever could in my old job. In fact, even though I fumbled my way through the day trading game for the first six months, I managed to make as much money by the eighth month that I used to make in a whole year at my old job! I must give a lot of credit to my friend Jeff, who was a massive help. I had called him up a few days after our run-in and told him of my interest in getting into day trading. He offered his support without hesitation. I am forever grateful to him because he was a great mentor—like a coach—to me. I am sure that without his spark, I might not have felt that fire inside me and pursued this career. He guided me by telling me how to get started and divide up the money for my trades. And that's why I created this book. I am passing on his good deed by helping as many new day traders as I can, including you!

Mind you, when I started my day trading journey, I got another job on the side, just to be safe. I'm not going to tell you something silly like quit your job. When you get the hang of things and find that you are making enough sustainable income from day trading, then you can rearrange your career to accommodate that. Day trading is just one of my multiple streams of income. Look at it as a way to diversify your portfolio.

To clarify, I don't want to sound like one of those gurus trying to reel you in by talking about how bad a 9 to 5 job is. There's nothing wrong with one. But, when you're stuck in a job you don't like and believe you're not living to your potential, it's time to do something about it.

My life has done a complete turnaround since I bumped into Jeff that day. I am confident that anyone and everyone can succeed as a day trader, just as he said, as long as they have the right tools. I did not even need a university degree in finance to get started. I didn't have to be a high-strung personality type like I used to think was the best fit for this career.

I cannot even describe how satisfying my life is now. It's that good. I wake up with purpose and an eagerness to get up and get going. Remember how excited you used to feel on the first day of school? (Or maybe the last day of school for some people). That's how I feel every morning when I get out of bed. Till today, my mind is always thinking about building on my day trading career. The mental stimulation is like nothing else. Many people tell you to find the thing that excites your mind and do that. Day trading gives me super happy feelings. Giving this career a shot is so worth it, to feel even a little bit like I do every day.

Even though I'm happy and making good money now, my start with day trading was rough until I got into my groove. I made a lot of mistakes. It's a rite of passage in this job—everyone learns by making mistakes. But there are steps you can follow, and they can help you make fewer uncostly mistakes. This book will be your primary tool and introduction to learning the process and make as few mistakes as possible. This can also be a great read that makes an excellent gift for anyone looking for ideas, inspiration, wisdom and encouragement.

THE FUNDAMENTALS

Making the Difference with Understanding

CHAPTER 1: INTO THE WORLD OF DAY TRADING

THE BENEFITS OF DAY TRADING

When they learn about this career correctly, a day trader can make a lot of money. There are many day traders earning millions of dollars in profits every year. That fact leads me to the greatest benefits of day trading; the things that can help someone gain financial freedom. This might sound harsh, but I felt like a financial slave before I became a day trader. I was trading my time for pay that was not enough to reach the life and goals I wanted. My chains were not physical; instead, they were mental. I thought I needed to struggle in that job I was in to get by. I didn't know I could do better.

I wasn't alone. Many people have to force themselves to get out of bed every day to go to a job they dislike. We have been brought up to think that this is the way it should be, and so people do not try very hard to break away from that type of mental slavery. That's what life is. In fact, most people don't even know they are slaves to that kind of system. When I'm talking about a financial or mental slave, I'm talking about people who are in a job they don't like and think that's the only way to live. They don't believe they can have a different life.

Before we go any further, I want to make something clear again. There's nothing wrong with working, what people call, a '9 to 5 job' if you're happy. People have different goals and priorities in life. Many want a simple life with a regular job. Others want more but don't have the confidence to pursue something different. If you're not living the life you want, make a change. Day trading is one of those careers that can allow you to make money. And, that extra money can allow you to pursue a different, more satisfying, life and career without the risk that comes with switching jobs.

With day trading, you can work to get financial independence that lets you be the one in control of your future, your destiny. That's not as farfetched as it might seem. You can have the stability of a satisfying career that does not chain you to a particular location or to specific times that you have to be working. I now travel when I want to, come and go as I need, and enjoy a quality of life that I could never have had at my old job. That is the power of financial freedom, and you can have a life like that too. Day trading can give you the ability to control your time, money and life.

This is not the only great thing about becoming a day trader. More benefits include:

- **It's easy to get started.** Yes, there is a lot to learn initially, but almost anyone can become a day trader. You do not need special education, nor do

19

you need to take any fancy course. You just need to be dedicated, focused, and willing to learn. Does that sound like you?

- **There is no limit to the amount that you can earn.** There's no maximum income that you can make with day trading. It all depends on your commitment and the skills you develop.

- **You can make money fast.** Because of the short-term nature of day trades, you can start making money from the first day you become an active day trader.

- **Profits can build quickly.** This is because day traders participate in several trades every day and do not make profits on only one trade.

- **It is an exciting career.** I work from home, yet a thrill gets my blood pumping every day as I analyze the stock market and make trades. The stock market changes so much, and so quickly that it gets my mind working hard, and there is never a dull moment.

ARE THERE DISADVANTAGES TO DAY TRADING?

There are downsides to everything, and the same truth applies to day trading. As part of giving, you a realistic look at what it means to be a day trader, I will also list the possible disadvantages:

- **There is the potential for big losses**. Just like you can make unlimited profits as a day trader, that goes for losing money, too. But this is usually a trap that untrained day traders fall into. By knowing how to handle the risks and your position, you can minimize those losses and maximize your profits.

- **It costs you some money to get started with day trading**. A day trader needs to have a brokerage account (*see Chapter 5*), which has to be loaded with a specific amount of money to trade.

- **Trading fees can add up**. Since the day trader performs several trades in a day, the cost of doing business can add up because you have to pay fees for every trade made.

- With day trading, I've discovered that doing the job correctly decreases the risks of working in this career. I will teach you how to set up that management system in this book as well.

IS DAY TRADING RIGHT FOR YOU?

After reading my story, I am sure you are asking yourself this because it's a question I often get from people contemplating day trading as a career. I will tell you what I always tell them: the truth is that I cannot answer that question for you. Only you can answer it after you have looked at the pros and cons, which I will talk about in the next chapter. However, I can tell you the number one quality you need to be a successful day trader: You need to have an entrepreneurial mindset. That means you are ready and willing to motivate yourself to do your work instead of having someone else tell you what you need to do next. You are your own boss as a day trader. There will be no one to dictate your schedule, but you must make yourself work hard to do what needs to be done. By doing that, you'll earn as much money as you want!

As an effective entrepreneur, you need to be:

- Good at managing your time.

- Willing to learn new things all the time.

- Accountable and responsible for yourself and your actions.

- Willing to take on new challenges.

- Self-aware and aware of the external world and events going on around you.

- Clear about your goals and how you are going to reach them.

- Good at creating systems that will give you direction.

One way to find out if day trading is for you is to ask yourself if you can think like a boss instead of like an employee. I hope that your answer is yes because endless possibilities are waiting at the end of that answer. The great thing about being an entrepreneur is that you do not have to have all the winning qualities right off the bat. In fact, most great entrepreneurs did not have all the best qualities and habits at the beginning of their venture into this lifestyle. What you need to start is a willingness to change and to learn. Everything else will fall into place after that. I never imagined myself as a business owner before. Still, I have completely changed my outlook on myself and my life after becoming a day trader. The journey inspired me to explore other ventures. Now, I own several other businesses in addition to being a day trader.

WHAT YOU WILL DISCOVER IN THIS BOOK

I am a straightforward guy, so you will find that I like to get right to the point. There will be no beating around the bush. I will not spout out terms at you like this is a textbook. All the words in this book are meant to be understood by a complete newbie. In addition to what has been covered above, you will learn:

- What day trading is (I thought that would be an excellent place to start!)

- How day trading differs from other types of trading

- What it means to be a day trader and what it takes to get started

- The basic rules of day trading

- Technical terms and phrases you need to know

- The ins and outs of high-frequency trading

- Why risk management is essential and how to manage your risk effectively

- Day trading strategies and analysis

- Much more!

Before we get to these explanations, one thing needs to be stated: day trading is a business. I will remind you that throughout this book, it's such an important thing to understand. Companies do not just spring up and become successful overnight, even though it sometimes appears that way to outsiders. Businesses take hours of devotion every day and months of behind-the-curtain work to become successful. In the case of day trading, it usually takes between 3 and 6 months of regular time and effort to get your feet firmly planted on the ground to see the results you want.

Day trading is not a get-rich-quick scheme. If you do not have the time it takes to learn the business's ins and outs, this is not your career. In fact, you must commit the right amount of time, be able to handle a challenge or the excitement of an ever-changing career, and have the will to learn and grow.

Join our community and learn from others. We learn the best when connecting and sharing with other peoples.

I invite you to join our community on Facebook. You can join at this link bit.ly/NoobsTradingFacebook and let's all live to our potential together.

Are you ready to be serious about gaining new tools and skills that will allow you to take control of your financial future? If so, then read on! I promise that this book will let you hit the ground running with day trading, even though you are starting with zero knowledge and experience.

Don't wait and miss out on the opportunity to take control of your finances and your life. Procrastination will keep you chained to financial slavery. Read this book in its entirety to see how YOU can be the master of your destiny!

We have a lot of ground to cover in a few pages. So, let's get started.

CHAPTER 2: THE BASICS OF DAY TRADING

WHAT IS DAY TRADING?

Day trading is the act of buying and selling assets (usually stocks) in the short term, within the space of a day. Day trading does not just deal with buying and selling stocks, though. Day traders also invest in other types of stock market assets, such as futures and forex. Futures are contracts worth money because they are from a particular asset such as oil or corn. This type of agreement indicates that the contract owner has to buy or sell that exact asset on a specific date for a price that was decided ahead of time. Futures are different from options, which also start from a financial contract. The buyer does not have to buy or sell the specified asset at the agreed-upon date with options. The owner of the contract—the buyer—only does so if it will benefit him or her. Consider a producer of an oil-based product acquiring a futures contract from an oil producer. This could be done to lock in the price so that they will not pay more for oil if the price changes unfavorably.

Forex stands for foreign exchange. This type of asset is exchanged on a market that is separate from the stock market. It involves buying and selling global currencies—money that comes from all different parts of the world. The forex market is even larger than the stock market. It's the world's most liquid financial market, which means buying and selling can be done quickly and easily.

The trader aims to make money on every trade. Because of the short-term nature of day trading, the amount of profit you can make on one trade is not usually very high. The trader does several transactions in a day so that the profit compounds or builds. You'll understand what this means in later chapters.

Some day traders dabble in the career part-time, but the most outstanding returns are only possible through full-time day trading. Nevertheless, it might be in your best interests as a newbie day trader to start part-time. If you do that, you cannot check in here and there or do the job on and off between other tasks in your life. Day trading is a serious commitment that needs your undivided attention at all times, not hurried check-ins.

This is a challenging career, like other new career paths. I am not here to tell you that you will earn millions of dollars within the first month with little to no effort. You could, but not right off the bat. That would be a completely false statement. Instead, if you choose this career, expect to put in a lot of time and effort right from the start. There is a steep learning curve, meaning there is a lot to learn at first. Don't get scared off, but you will lose money. You'll do it smartly, though, as you discover within this book. All traders do, no matter how experienced they are or what stage they are in their careers. That doesn't mean failure. It's just part of the biz.

The reason you have to give so much time and work to day trading is that the stock market and other financial markets are very unpredictable. Market conditions can change at the drop of a hat, so where a day trader might have believed that he or she would make a profit in a short period of time, that may no longer be the case. The day trader needs to be prepared for these quick changes in market conditions and react just as quickly to make sure they still have profits and lose as little as possible. That swift reaction time means the day trader needs to be on the ball at all trading day hours. So, popping your head in and out of day trading will likely lead to more losses than wins.

Check out my infographic of a day in the life of a day trader. It gives you an idea of how day traders structure their day. Visit this link to download it: bit.ly/Noobsinfographic.

STOCKS AND THE STOCK MARKET

First thing's first. If you're going to be a day trader, you need to understand the stock market because that is where most of the trades happen. Chapter 3 goes more into detail about the stock market, but let's touch on it now. Imagine walking into a cafeteria and buying a slice of pizza. The server has a whole pizza, and he takes out one piece and hands it to you. Buying stocks is a little like that—except instead of a pizza, it's a company. Stocks represent ownership in a company, so buying stock means buying a piece of a company. Each piece bought is called a share. Owners of shares are called shareholders. As a shareholder, a person benefits when a company performs profitably, as it makes money. When it's performing well, the price of its stock goes up, so as a shareholder, you can sell that stock for a higher price than you bought it for, and voila! You make a profit. The reverse is also true, and then you lose money; that's why you have to properly analyze the stock and the company before trading in that stock. I will reveal how to do this within this book.

Ownership of certain types of shares has other benefits, too, like the payment of dividends to the shareholder. That means, as a shareholder, you get paid when owning shares in particular companies. Dividends are regular payments distributed among shareholders. These payments are typically distributed quarterly—every three months—are for the same amount and are based on the company's profits or cash reserves.

Take one example, the company called Three-M Co. declared dividend payments of $1.47 per share on November 10, 2020. It also announced the same dividend amount payment for shareholders 3 months before that on August 13, 2020.

Shareholders can also make more in the form of earnings. Earnings are another type of payment made to shareholders based on profits that the company has made over a specific time. Let's say that company ABC made gross sales of $1,000,000 in 2019. The company spent $100,000 on operation costs, $500,000 on the cost of goods sold (cost of creating the products sold that year and had to pay taxes of $50,000. Taking all that away from $1,000,000 leaves us with $350,000. $350,000 is the earnings, which is the company's net profit, which can be distributed to shareholders. But management makes the call on what to do with the net income each year. They can either pay a cash dividend or keep the earnings for use in the business.

There are different types of stocks, which decide the benefits a shareholder will receive from ownership of those shares. No matter the kind of stock a shareholder owns, stocks are a powerful investment tool for a few reasons:

- **The high liquidity of stock.** Liquidity refers to how easily an asset can be bought and sold without a significant cost placed on the transaction. The reason the stocks can be liquid is the fact that so many other people are trading the stock daily. It's easier to sell because of demand. Highly liquid stocks can be bought and sold without the price being harshly affected. Imagine a trader sold 100 shares of stock for $30.00 per share. If they received $29.51 per share by the time the transaction was complete that same day, this would have been a highly liquid stock. On the other hand, if the stock is illiquid (opposite of liquid), you'd have to accept that the stock would drop to accommodate your sale. Illiquid can also signify that there isn't much interest in the stock, so it might be more challenging to sell.

- **Traders can earn high profits over a short period.** The nature of stocks is that they can change in price in as little as a few minutes, so day traders can profit from trading them in less than a day.

- **Allowance for creating a diverse portfolio.** A portfolio shows the different kinds of assets that a person has built up. An ideal portfolio makes sure that a trader does not have all his or her eggs in one basket. In other words, he or she should have a variety of different types of investments, such as stock, real estate and options. Stock investment helps because there are many industries, sectors, and markets that a trader can invest in to ensure diversification. For example, the trader can have that diversity by investing in stock in the health care, technology and utility industries.

- **Allowance ownership in big-name companies.** You can have a say in how a company performs and potentially earn the other benefits stated. Being a shareholder in a construction company may give voting rights to whether this company will add another product or service to its list for sale to customers.

- **Convenience.** Computers and the Internet have made it easy for anyone to operate on the stock market. With that, all a trader needs is a way to make online payments.

Stocks traded on the stock market are securities. Securities are also known as tradable financial assets (cash, stocks, bonds, mutual funds, bank deposits, options, and EFTs) and are exchanged in the market. The terms' definitions can be found in the *Terms and Phrases* section of this chapter and throughout the book. If you want to find a particular word, locate it using the index at the end of the book. As you can see, a trader can trade many other assets on the market, not just stock. The stock market is a highly diverse industry. Remember the word *security*. I'll be using this word a lot throughout this book to refer to tradable financial assets, as we've just discussed.

Popular global stock markets include:

- The New York Stock Exchange (NYSE)

- The NASDAQ (National Association of Securities Dealers Automated Quotations)

- London Stock Exchange

- Hong Kong Stock Exchange

- Shanghai Stock Exchange

- Euronext

Companies list the securities that they would like traded on these markets, and traders have the option to pick up these securities for a price. Stock markets operate like auction houses, so buyers and sellers negotiate before settling on a price. Once this agreement is made, a trade is transacted. Let's say a company may have listed stock for sale at $20 per share. While one trader may have offered the company the price they listed, the company could sell to the trader that offered to purchase the stock at $22 per share. A company doesn't usually change the price of securities on a buyer (a security's value is dependent on the market). Still, if a buyer offers a higher price than listed, the company is likely to sell to that buyer instead. Investments are basically placing bids on the securities, and the best bid wins. Think about it like this, if you're selling your used PlayStation 4, there's a market value for it, so you'd probably sell it at around that price. But you're most likely going to sell it to the highest bidder if given the opportunity.

How to Start Day Trading

You cannot benefit from the stock market or ownership in companies if you do not set the groundwork. The first thing you do is take a good look at your current financial position. You have to do this because trading on the stock market is a risk. Just as you stand to profit, losses can and will result. But experiencing losses are the only way you'll learn, and you can learn how to lose in a smart way. Therefore, the money you put up for investing needs to be money you can afford to lose. Please don't do it like some people and put up all your savings. You need to have separate savings and investing funds. I cannot stress this enough—never, ever invest in assets that you cannot afford to lose because you'll be in a massive jam if trades do not work out in your favor. There were times where I lucked out with my reckless moves, and other times I didn't. Still, I have heard many horror stories of traders losing significantly because of reckless trading strategies and actions.

It's never wise to jump into the deep end of the stock market pool without experience. Therefore, the smart thing to do is paper trade. Paper trading (also known as simulated trade) uses real-life happenings on the stock market to practice and determine how you would play

34

out the trade. This safely allows novice day traders to get their feet wet without risking real money. Some websites and apps allow you to paper trade easily online. One such example is TD Ameritrade Think Or Swim's Paper Money. You can also easily find more on the web to find the one that works best for you.

Practice getting a handle on the stock market. You'll figure out strategies that work and those that don't. When you have determined that you are ready to start day trading, you can get set up with a brokerage firm. Think of brokerage firms as the middleman between the trader and the stock market. They represent traders, and that is required to get started as a day trader. However, you cannot just go to one and get signed up. There is a qualification process that you do. Depending on the evaluation results, you're placed at an appropriate level based on your trading experience.

Not all day trades need a broker or a required minimum amount, which you'll learn later in the book, but there are instances where you would need one or both of those.

Once you are sure that you have a safe investment pool of funds, which could be a minimum of $25,000 in the USA, you can move onto practicing day trading. Before I explain this point, let's take a moment to discuss the amount of money you might need to be a day trader. While the $25,000 requirement stands in the USA, it varies from country to country, and quick research online will give you more answers. For example, there is no required minimum amount to day trade in Canada, but maybe a brokerage firm might require a day trader to hold a certain amount in their brokerage account to allow day trades. You should follow up with the broker you decide to work with to ensure that you meet the minimum requirements. If you trade with a cash account only, it's possible to trade without a $25,000 requirement in your account. But, there is still risk in doing so, and you're at a considerable disadvantage because you are limited to two or three-day trades per week. As you begin trading, all this will start making sense.

You should note that you do not have to use the entire amount in your account in day-to-day trades. If day trading stocks are too pricy for you, you can start trading futures instead. The minimum account balance for trading that security is usually $1000.

The information in this book leans mostly toward stocks, but day traders trade stocks, options, futures, commodities, foreign currencies (forex), and/or cryptocurrencies. They all have different requirements or minimum account balance requirements, and some don't. But, as I said, it varies from country to country, so depending on where you are, you'd have to do a quick search to find out.

Depending on what you're trading, it's always smart to have a minimum account balance. The amount varies on what you're trading. I suggest asking someone who has experience in a particular security you're interested in.

Once you have been qualified as a trader, you will set up two types of accounts with your brokerage firm. These accounts arc necessary to facilitate trades, meaning you will not be able to trade anything until they are set up correctly. The first type of account is called a cash account, which, as the name suggests, allows the trader to transact trades using cash. The other type of account is called a margin account. This account allows the trader to make trades backed by the value of other securities that he or she owns. In essence, the trader is trading on money borrowed from the broker. It's a loan that needs to be paid back with interest. I know all this stuff might seem like a lot of information, but things will start making more sense the further you get into the book. You can go back to this section later, and I promise you'll understand it better.

Choosing a brokerage firm is a big deal, and you should not just contact the first one you stumble across. Please do your research about the features that the firm offers, the fees it charges to represent traders, and how quickly it allows trades to occur, to name a few of the considerations. Luckily, most brokers are set up online, so you don't have to walk into a brick-and-mortar location to get the representation you need.

BASIC RULES OF DAY TRADING

After you have gotten set up with your brokerage firm, it's time to start trading. Feeling lost? I was too in the early stages of my day trading career. At its most basic, day trading is about reading stocks and understanding how the stock market moves. That is the only way to make a profit. To help you get started, here are a few guidelines to help you get through the trading process:

- **Educate yourself and always stay informed**. You're in a new and exciting world, but you need to look both ways before you ever consider entering a trade. Learn all you can about the companies you are thinking about investing in. Track how the stock market performs overall, watch the news to see what's happening in politics, if any natural disasters have occurred, etc. There is no shortage of things that can affect how stocks perform, and knowledge of those things allows you to gain power. Never trust unreliable sources about stocks. Your uncle Chester might know more about pig farming than anyone you know. But that doesn't mean you should load up on beet stocks just because he told you he heard their price was going to go up because his neighbor's beet farm had a flood, and they lost half their crop. Always do your own research.

- **Learn to use the tools of the trade.** Choosing the right stock to trade means that you have to do some homework beforehand. Tools like line charts help you get the job done because you can look for clues in the graphs' trends.

- **Have realistic expectations.** As I've said, there is great potential for profits in day trading, but those profits do not fall out of a hat and land at your feet. Some of the most successful day traders are men and women who have paid their dues by making mistakes and losing money. They are reaping the rewards of their persistence, consistency, and commitment to the career. Do not fall into the trap of thinking that you will earn millions in your first month of day trading.

- **Always have an entry and an exit strategy when considering trades.** Your entry strategy includes the amount of money you would like to offer for the stock in question and how much profit you would like to make off that trader. Your exit strategy includes deciding what price you would like to sell the stock for and what condition needs to be in place for you to cut your losses and back out of the trade. You'll learn more about this later in the book.

- **Keep trading on margin to a minimum**. While using the margin account can lead to a trader being in a better position while trading, the losses can also be more significant if the trade does not work out in the trader's favor.

- **Keep a journal of all your trades.** This allows you to note the strategies that work and those you need to improve on. The great thing about experiencing losses is that you learn from your mistakes, so they hopefully don't happen again.

TERMS AND PHRASES

Before we move on to the more technical aspects of day trading, let us go over a few new terms and phrases. Also, we'll review those that we discussed above. Every career and field has its particular language, and if you do not want to be left in the dark, you'll want to know the jargon of day trading. These are excellent terms and phrases to start with, and there will be more later in the book. If you don't understand these terms, don't worry. They will be covered more in-depth later in the book.

- **Bearish conditions**: This is a state of decreasing prices of the stock market.

- **Bonds**: Unlike stocks, bonds can be taken on by a trader or investor while earning interest.

- **Break-even**: The condition wherein a trader makes neither a loss nor a profit from a trade.

- **Bullish conditions**: This is a state of increasing prices of the stock market.

- **Derivative contract**: This is a financial contract that derives its value based on the asset's cost attached to the contract.

- **ETF**: This is an acronym for Exchange-Traded Fund and is a mixed investment of stocks and mutual funds.

- **Interest rate**: This is a percentage charged for using borrowed money over a specific amount of time.

- **Mutual funds**: These are funds collected from multiple investors, companies, or other entities for investment, to spread the risk of the investment.

As an extra bonus, I have some flashcards of terms and definitions you can practice. There are many we have covered in this book, plus more. You'll learn faster. Visit this link for the flashcards: bit.ly/NoobsTradingDefinitions.

BONDS

Let me quickly define bonds. A bond is basically a loan. It's given to a company or government by an investor. By granting a bond, a company or government can borrow money from an investor like yourself. In exchange, you are paid interest on the money they've given out. So, you get your money back when you let companies or governments borrow your money, plus you get interest payments on top of that loan. Doesn't that sound dope? Why do Companies and governments issue bonds? They do it as often as possible to finance new projects or ongoing costs.

Investors may use bonds, hoping to secure the money they have while generating extra income. They are frequently seen as a less risky pick than stocks. Bonds are utilized to expand a portfolio. Since they offer routinely scheduled payments and the return of invested principal, bonds are regularly seen as a more foreseeable and stable form of investing.

Compare standard payments of a bond to the case of owning a stock. With stocks, profits and losses are driven by market forces and are, for the most part, difficult to forecast. Of course, like any investment, bonds are not without risk. One risk that bond investors face is the possibility that the issuer (the company or government) defaults on paying back the money you put into the bond. This is usually known as default risk. Ordinarily, bonds with higher default risk also come with higher coupon rates. Coupon rate refers to the interest paid by a bond issuer. The sum of risk depends for the most part on the financial steadiness of the issuer. For instance, most governments are, for the most part, considered stable issuers and issue bonds with a generally low coupon rate. Corporate bonds generally present a more prominent risk of default, as companies can and do go bankrupt. That's why corporate bonds regularly offer a higher coupon rate.

The good news is credit rating agencies rank different bonds. This could offer assistance to bond speculators to gauge the financial strength of the bond issuer. When considering a particular bond, it's best to compare ratings. These rating agencies use different criteria when measuring risk.

A mix of stocks and bonds are what many investors pursue. This helps increase and protect portfolio returns because bonds move differently than stocks. All in all, you might consider bonds as capital preservation and income generation.

If you are thinking this has *got* to be the end of all the terms related to day trading, well, good news! There are many more terms, and they will be covered throughout this book.

CHAPTER SUMMARY

- Day trading is the act of buying and selling assets on financial markets like the stock market within the space of a day.

- Stocks are one of the main assets traded in day trading.

- Stocks represent ownership in a company (remember the pizza?) and are traded on the stock market.

- In many cases, a minimum account balance requirement of $25,000 is needed in the USA to fund a brokerage account to allow day trades, but it varies from country to country. Not all securities need a minimum of $25,000 to day trade with.

- A minimum account balance requirement depends on what security you're trading. Day traders can trade stocks, options, futures, commodities, foreign currencies (forex), or cryptocurrencies.

CHAPTER 3: THE STOCK MARKET

Stocks and the stock market… Let's retake a look at them. Think of them as the fruits that nourish your bank account and the supermarket where you are guaranteed to get the best pick. These are typically the first two concepts that traders of all types are introduced to at the beginning of this career journey. Stocks are a type of security. A security is simply a tradeable financial asset. Even though very popular, stocks are just one type of financial asset that can be traded on the stock market.

Learn *how to research a stock before trading*, have a greater understanding about the *overview of the stock market*, and *more*. You can download my magazine for free as a gift at this link bit.ly/NoobsMagazine.

THERE ARE THREE TYPES OF SECURITIES

They are:

- **Equity securities**, which are financial instruments that give ownership rights to the person who purchases them. Stocks are an example of equity security. They are a representation of ownership in an entity such as a partnership, company, or trust. Think of shares as buying a piece of a company or other entity.

The person who owns the stock is called a shareholder. This is because stocks are sold in batches called shares, which are typically in groups of 100. Just like you never buy one egg but rather a dozen at a time, stocks come as packaged deals. There are two types of stocks, and they are called common and preferred stock. A trader owns a piece of the company when purchasing common stocks, and so has a say in what goes in by way of voting rights.

On the other hand, while having voting rights is not a standard feature of preferred stocks, they allow traders to earn extra income through dividend payments. Dividends are sums of money shared among the stockholders of a company. This is usually distributed every 3 months. Think of it as receiving a free gift for making a purchase at a store. Most traders are more enticed by the idea of the extra income attached to preferred stock.

- **Debt securities**, which are financial assets that need to be paid back in periodic payments. In essence, they are loans that must be paid back with interest and other terms like a maturity or renewal date. It's like paying your best friend's mortgage for him or her then receiving that monthly amount plus a percentage of that amount in repayment. Popular types of debt securities include corporate and government bonds and certificates of deposit.

- **Hybrid securities**, which are financial assets that combine characteristics of the first two types of securities (equity and debt securities). Examples of hybrid securities include equity warrants and convertible bonds. Equity warrants represent the option that a shareholder has to buy shares of stock from a company within a certain amount of time. In particular, if a company offers a stock warrant that allows a trader to buy stocks for $15 per share over the next ten years, the trader can still purchase the stock for this price of $15. Even though it might have changed value and is worth $350 or any other value. Convertible bonds are bonds that can be converted into shares of common stock. Convertible bonds are represented by a ratio. For example, a 5:1 convertible bond means that 1 bond will be converted into 5 shares of stock. It's like a gift that keeps on giving. Remember how we talked about bonds in chapter 2? You can loan a government or company money, and you can get it back, plus interest. Instead of getting your money back, you'd get stock in the company instead. That's how convertible bonds work.

Like I said, these stock markets operate like auction houses. *Going once, going twice, sold to the highest bidder...* Think of that kind of energy when you think of the stock market. Sellers of securities like companies list securities on these stock markets and then negotiate with buyers on selling these stocks at an agreed-upon price. Once these two parties come to an agreement, a trade is made.

The stock market is regulated by government authorities to ensure everything remains on the up and up. Both sellers and buyers are treated fairly. The authority responsible for this in the United States is called the US Securities and Exchange Commission (SEC).

OTHER FINANCIAL MARKETS

A financial market, like the stock market, is a marketplace where financial assets are traded. Day traders do not just operate on the stock market. Other financial markets where they can make profitable trades include:

FOREIGN EXCHANGE (FOREX) MARKET

This market doesn't have one physical location and is decentralized. As the world's largest financial market, it operates every day without an opening or closing time. This market is focused on the trading of currencies (or money) all over the world.

CRYPTOCURRENCY MARKET

This market is a relatively new financial market that emerged in the last few decades. It revolves around the exchange of digital and cryptocurrency (we'll get to what that means later). Because of the enormous profits potentially earned from this financial market, it is being utilized by experienced and novice traders despite its infancy.

DERIVATIVES MARKET

This financial market is where trades are made based on the value derived from contracts, hence the market's name. Therefore, let's say that Company X produces cotton t-shirts. Cotton is the main item needed to produce these shirts, and so they need a consistent supply that is priced in a way that allows them to meet their bottom line every month. As a result, this company enters a derivative agreement with Company C, a cotton supplier, that allows Company X to purchase cotton at a specific monthly price. Even if the price of cotton rises on the market. Company X has to pay a premium for this contract, say $1500 but has the protection of purchasing cotton for the specified price for the term of the contract, which we will place as 10 years for the example. Company C also gains security from this contract as the company is guaranteed the income of the specified number of bales that Company X will be purchasing monthly. Furthermore, For the sake of the example, let's say 1000 bales of cotton will be purchased by Company X monthly, priced at $100 each. Therefore, the price of this derivative contract is based on the premium paid by Company X plus the specified purchase made monthly for 10 years by Company X. The value of the contract is $1,001,500.

COMMODITIES MARKET

This financial market is where traders buy and sell natural resources and commodities like gold, corn, and oil.

THE ROLE OF FINANCIAL MARKETS

You might be wondering why these financial markets are so important. You might even be thinking that they're a concept that rich folk invented just to pass money around, and you will not be the first to think that. But financial markets are far more than that. They help drive the national and global economy. The financial markets facilitate this in a variety of ways, and these ways include:

- Helping persons put their savings into productive use instead of just sitting in a bank account. Of course, savings need to be had, but having a too large pool can be more of a handicap than a useful resource. The financial markets are a way to get more out of your savings. In other words, they allow a person to potentially earn more than they would have off the interest earned on the same amount of money in a savings account. As a model, if a person started off with an initial deposit of $100 and made a monthly contribution of $200 every month for 10 years, this person could end up with $25,334.65 with a savings account, which provides a 1% interest rate. The usual range of interest rate in the US is between 0.01% and 1.75%.

- Allowing securities to be liquid (easy to convert to cash or to change hands). Namely, stocks that are traded in day trades are clearly highly liquid because they make traders' profits (are converted into cash) in the space of hours or even minutes. Without the playing field that the financial markets provide, many financial assets would not be able to change hands so effortlessly (or be so liquid). Therefore, finances would not flow through the economy smoothly, and thus, this would stagnate the economy.

- Lowering the cost of trading financial assets. Imagine having to individually approach each of the companies whose securities you'd like to trade. In that complicated imaginary world, you would likely have to hire legal help and other professionals to initiate and follow through with these trades. The costs would quickly add up with this method and cut on potential profits. Because the financial markets provide that playing field for exchanges, this allows for the lowered cost of doing those transactions by limiting them to common fees like commission fees.

- Aiding in determining the price of financial assets. It would be hard to keep track of if you were getting a fair price of securities offered by companies. Unless there was an easily accessible place where you could compare securities. Like other marketplaces, securities prices are typically determined by supply and demand in the financial markets, ensuring fairness in trades.

- Helping lower the national unemployment rate because it offers job opportunities to a variety of people. The more traders and investors buy stocks and other securities from companies, the more they can invest in growth. The more companies grow, the more positions are filled up, and thus, employment rates go up.

- Allowing companies, government organizations, and individuals to have access to additional capital.

The best thing about the financial market's financial drive is that it gives both sellers and buyers an even playing field for fair treatment and access to resources.

That means that anyone, people like you and I, have the same access that everyone does to the same resources in the financial markets (regardless of the level of wealth anyone has).

CHAPTER SUMMARY

- There are specific steps that a novice must go through to learn the best applications when it comes to day trading, and the first step is arming his or herself with knowledge. Knowledge about stocks and the stock market is essential to obtain.

- Stocks are a type of security, which simply is a tradable financial asset. And, there are three types of securities: equity securities, debt securities, and hybrid securities. Stocks are equity securities.

- Stocks are traded on the stock markets, but the stock market goes by another name: securities exchange; because such a wide array of securities are exchanged there. Popular global stock markets include the NASDAQ (National Association of Securities Dealers Automated Quotations), The New York Stock Exchange (NYSE), and the London Stock Exchange.

- The stock market is only one type of financial market where day traders can participate in trades. Other types of financial markets where day traders can find trading opportunities include the foreign exchange (forex) market and the cryptocurrency market.

- Financial markets are essential for developing the economy on both a national and global level. They facilitate this by helping persons put their savings into productive use, allowing securities to be liquid, lowering the cost of trading financial assets, aiding in determining the price of financial assets, helping lower the national unemployment rate and allowing companies (government organizations and individuals) to have access to additional capital.

- The best thing about the financial market's financial drive is that it gives both sellers and buyers an even playing field for fair treatment and access to resources. That means that anyone can have the same access to the same resources in the financial markets.

THE 1ST LAW

The Power in the Process

CHAPTER 4: HOW DAY TRADING WORKS

DAY TRADING VS. OTHER TYPES OF TRADING

The stock markets are enormous, with thousands of companies listed and even more securities listed under each of them. With so many choices, I'm sure you can believe me when I tell you there is more than one way to approach trading on the stock market. So, why is day trading fantastic? Let's look at the different trading methods and how day trading stacks up against the rest.

Position trading is the first type of trading that we'll look at... It's also called the buy and hold strategy. Unlike day trading, this is not active trading whereby the trader gets in the thick of things. Instead, the trader holds the securities for a long time, typically months or years. This method of trading relies on the price of the security moving over the long term.

For this reason, the trader can ignore the short-term fluctuations of prices of the security. While this trading style allows for greater profits, it can also limit the trader because a loss can still result. It could take the trader a long time to come to that conclusion.

Swing trading is another type of trading style... Swing traders only participate in the stock market when they notice a trend that they can benefit from. This trend usually comes about when prices are unstable and hard to predict. So, the buying and selling of stock and other securities are based on that trend. Swing traders usually operate in the short term, and trades are generally done in one day or less. So, even though the swing trader does not make trades on a day-to-day basis like a day trader, they still need to regularly monitor the stock market to know when to ride a trend. Like a surfer waits to catch the right wave. As a case in point, while a day trader can enter and exit a trade in a matter of minutes, the swing trader may exit a new trade 2 weeks after entry. I will touch on swing trading again further in the book.

Also, check out my book on swing trading! bit.ly/SwingTradingForNoobs

Scalping is the final type of trading style that we will discuss … scalping is a quick trading style that makes profits based on small movements in prices. Scalpers do not try to make a profit on significant gaps in prices. Unlike swing trading, which relies on a highly volatile stock market, successful scalping depends on a quiet stock market. Let me give you an example with numbers. Don't worry too much if you don't get it right away. The further you read in the book, the more you'll understand. Let's look at a scalping trader who makes a profit by buying a massive number of stock shares from a company at $15 per share. Say he or she sell these shares of stock for $15.10 at opportune moments. That means the trader makes a small profit of $0.10 of each share of stock. Doesn't sound like much. But, what if the trader had bought and sold 25,000 shares of that stock. That means they paid a total of $375,000 and could now sell them for $377,500. He or she would have made a profit of $2500.

Of all these trading strategies, day trading is the best-known and most widely-used trading form on the stock market. This is because its role is highly active, not passive, like position trading. The high level of activity is what allows for gaining results the very same day.

Traditionally, day trading was done by specialists on the stock market, but electronic trading has made it more accessible. Now, every day, people like you and me can benefit from the stock market. Some of the most popular and trusted online day trading platforms include:

- E*TRADE

- Fidelity

- TradeStation

- TD Ameritrade

RETAIL VS. INSTITUTIONAL TRADERS

Just as there are different types of trading, there are also other types of traders. Traders fall into two basic categories: retail and institutional. Institutional traders enter trades to manage financial markets' transactions on behalf of a group of people, a company, or some other formal entity. Typical types of trading accounts that institutional traders manage include insurance companies, exchange-traded funds, and pension funds. I mean, this might be exciting stuff for some people!

In the past, institutional traders definitely had a leg up in the financial markets. Times are changing, though (as they always are). The advantages institutional traders once had had been eroding due to advances in technology. This has allowed people to trade on all financial markets of the world from any location. Currently, retail traders have just as many benefits as institutional traders. Retail traders are individuals who manage personal trading accounts.

There are some advantages that only institutional traders can get in the financial markets. They can negotiate the fees of trading and have better access to particular securities, such as futures. Institutional traders typically have the option for better prices when trading securities compared to retail traders. Another massive benefit that institutional traders have over retail traders is called high-frequency trading. Also known as HFT, high-frequency trading uses computer programs to make many trades within seconds. The computer program allows for the analysis of many markets to find the best choices to invest and trade. When it finds these beneficial conditions, it sends out orders based on the current market conditions and future predictions that the program has made. All of this happens in fractions of a second, so the profit potential is enormous.

This information is essential for you because you will probably start off this career as a retail trader. While technology has allowed you ease of entry into this industry, there are a few cons you should know about. You'll face higher costs of doing business, especially since you have to go through a brokerage firm to enter and exit trades, unlike an institutional trader. However, the disadvantages do not take away from the fact that retail traders are significant players. They make the world's stock market and other financial markets as fluid as they are now. Retail traders take up more and more of the bulk of market trading activity, which is new and exciting.

BUYING LONG VS. SELLING SHORT

When I first heard these two terms, my mind conjured up a million complicated equations and difficult-to-understand explanations. Don't be like me! I caused myself senseless stress and tore out perfect, lustrous hair strands for no reason.

Buying long and selling short simply refers to whether a day trader enters a trade by buying or selling the asset first. You will need to be familiar with these two terms, regardless of the type of trading you choose to get into.

Buying long is when a day trader purchases the security specified in that trade with the expectation that the price will rise in the future so the trader can sell it and make a profit. Let's say that a day trader is interested in buying long by buying shares of stock from a particular company. Each share costs $10, so it will cost the day trader $10,000 to purchase 1,000 shares. The day trader sees potential for this stock to increase in value by at least $0.50 per share of stock. If this happens, the day trader will sell the stock for that amount and receive $10,500. Therefore, the day trader will make a profit of $500, minus any fees he has to pay for doing the transaction.

On the other hand, selling short is started by the day trader selling securities he intends to buy again later at a lower price to make a profit. Most newbie day traders are more confused about the concept of selling short than buying long. Still, it is just as easy to put into practice. An example is also fitting here to show you how this works. Let us keep our hypothetical situation whereby a day trader deals with 1,000 shares of stock from a particular company. The stock costs $10 per share. The day trader will start trading by selling these 1,000 shares of stock with the expectation that the price will go down so they can buy back that stock at a lower price. If the stock price goes down as predicted and costs $9.50 per share, then the day trader will pay $9,500 for the 1,000 shares of stock. Because the day trader paid $10,000 when initially entering the trade, they will now stand to profit by $500, minus the cost of doing that transaction. If the stock price had gone up as with the example for showing buying long, then the trader would have made a loss of $500 plus any fees associated with the transaction. I highly advise against selling short, especially when you're new to trading. I'll touch on that later in the book.

HOW TO FIND THE BEST TRADES

There is an art and a science to finding the best trades to participate in. You cannot just enter trades willy-nilly. Doing so would be an excellent way to lose more than you gain. While you do not have high-frequency trading on your side as a retail day trader, there are still several trade tools that make it easy to find profitable trades.

As a day trader, the focus is typically on highly volatile stocks. Volatility refers to how likely the price of stock, and other securities, are to change within a specific period. Securities with low volatility are usually very stable in price. Can you see how that could be a problem in day trading? Day traders *want* the price of assets to move up or down because such securities offer the best opportunity to make money in less than a day. These types of securities can even allow day traders to make profits in a matter of seconds!

You would need to do a technical analysis to find volatile stock. This will be covered in the next chapter. The good news is, you don't have to spend hours staring at a computer screen to figure out the best trade. A few qualities usually hint at high volatility with stock and other securities traded on the financial markets. Volume is one of the most essential qualities. Volume shows us how many traders are purchasing that particular type of security. High volume means there is a lot of interest in that security, which means it is easy to enter and exit trades. Volume is an indicator of liquidity. Remember liquidity? That's a measure of how quickly and easily an asset can be sold for cash. As we discussed earlier, securities with high liquidity are best for trading in the short term.

To sum it up, when looking at the stocks that are best for trading, avoid stocks and other securities that are low in volume and are not liquid (illiquid). You want highly volatile and liquid stocks.

CHAPTER SUMMARY

Day trading is only one type of trading. It is highly active compared to more passive trading methods like position trading and swing trading.

- There are different types of day traders. The first type is called institutional traders, and the other is called retail traders.

- Institutional traders enter trades to facilitate the management of transactions on behalf of a group of people, companies, or other formal entities.

- Retail traders are individuals who manage personal trading accounts.

- Both types of traders enter trades by buying long and selling short.

- Buying long is when a day trader purchases the security specified in a trade expecting that the price will rise.

- Selling short is done by selling the securities specified to purchase them again later at a lower price.

- The best stocks for day trading are highly volatile, high volume, and liquid.

I ask you, humbly, to help

Thank you and congratulations for reading up until this point.

Only 8% of readers ever leave a review, a large portion of purchases are inspired by reviews.

Do you mind taking a minute to write a review on www.amazon.com about this book?

I love to get feedback and check all my reviews (knowing that I'm helping people is the real pay for my work).

I thank you from the bottom of my heart.

CHAPTER 5: FIND THE BROKERS

Brokers are a necessary evil to deal with if you want to be a day trader without being evil yourself. Well, to put it straight, they are not as evil as long as they have a good reputation for caring for traders and handling trades. Broker and brokerage firms are terms you will hear a lot in this book because, in many cases, you'll need to have their representation if you want to be a day trader. You may need to transact with a broker with every trade you make, to be exact.

Therefore, it is prudent that we take the time to speak on what exactly a broker does. You can ensure that you get the best representation from the one you choose to work with.

UNDERSTANDING WHAT THE BROKER DOES

In essence, the broker or brokerage firm is a middleman between traders and the stock market. They are a door to the trading market. The broker is necessary because this is the person or company authorized to buy and sell stocks and other securities on the world's stock market and other financial markets. The broker is the one who places orders on behalf of day traders. Without the broker, the day trader would not make a profit because no transaction would be done.

To understand why the broker is such a necessary figurehead in the trading process, recognize that it works like an auction house. Just like the auctioneer acts as the middleman between buyers and sellers at an auction house, the broker also takes on the middleman's role between buyers and sellers on the financial market. You cannot just come up and pick up a stock or other security to buy or sell as you would fruit at the supermarket.

The stock markets have stock and other securities listed for buying and selling. Still, these come with rules and regulations that need to be adhered to if the stock market is to work like a finely tuned machine. One such government regulation is that companies that sell stocks publicly must make their financial statements public. This is so traders and investors can easily access them for fair transactions to occur.

These rules and regulations allow buyers and sellers to interact with each other in a civilized and coordinated manner. Otherwise, it will feel like a pack of wolves going in for the kill. Isn't that always the case when money is involved?

Prices on the stock market always change, influenced by factors like demand. Therefore, an entity needs to look out for the people's best interests and companies operating on the stock market. That entity is the broker. The broker makes it his business to know the stock markets' ins and outs and the rules and regulations that govern them.

Stock markets do not function like supermarkets, where you can just walk and pick up something off the shelf. It's rather like an auction house where the best bids win; the broker is placing those bids.

Not just anyone can become a broker, though. A broker needs to become licensed to execute trades on behalf of traders. In the U.S., the broker receives this license from the U.S. Securities and Exchange Commission.

Outside their function as representatives of traders on the stock markets, brokers sometimes offer traders advice on the best stock and other securities (in their opinion) to bid on. Do not only rely on brokers as your financial planner, though, or your sole guide for picking trades. Remember that you should have a sound plan and a solid strategy for picking the stock or other securities you bid on.

ALL SIDES OF BROKER SERVICES

The representation and guidance that a good broker can offer are invaluable, and as such, this comes at a cost. That's right. You need to pay a broker to get this excellent service. This should not come as a surprise since there is not much being offered for free in this world, especially if that service stands to make you millions of dollars within months.

There are two ways in which brokers earn compensation for their services. The first way is via a commission fee. A commission fee is a service charge defined by the broker as necessary for handling the execution of trade orders. Different brokers charge different commission fees. It is up to the trader to determine if the commission fee is worth it as a cost of doing business. Each trade order executed by the broker has a commission fee, which can add up quickly.

The other way brokers can earn compensation is by earning interest off the uninvested cash in a trader's accounts. A day trader typically cannot use all the cash in their cash (or margin) account. A small amount is always reserved. The broker uses that small amount by placing it in a deposit account to earn interest. Some of that interest is paid to the trader at the end of the investment period. The broker keeps the rest.

As mentioned earlier, brokers are a necessary evil that comes with the territory of day trading. I have come to accept the importance of their role in the day trading process and made peace with their fees. It will serve you well to do the same. Still, you need to protect yourself from getting ripped off. The next section will explain what to know before choosing a broker representation.

QUESTIONS BEFORE OPENING YOUR BROKERAGE ACCOUNT

It is a minefield out there, and even large brokers are going bust because the competition is so fierce these days. You must still choose the right broker representation for you because making the wrong choice could mean failing as a day trader. Here are a few questions that you need to ask yourself when searching for a broker, one of the first steps to becoming a money-making day trader:

Does the broker provide online services?

You can walk into a physical location to source a broker. Still, most brokers now offer online signup and services, which is a lot more convenient than trying to reach them through phone or other means.

What type of reputation does this broker have?

There are many scams out there now, which, unfortunately, extends to brokcr scrvices. Ensure that you do your research before signing up with a broker by ensuring that they have good reviews and a stellar level of expertise under their belt. Also, consider talking to someone who has used their service before.

What are the requirements for opening broker cash and margin accounts?

There are no two ways about it; you need a cash and margin account to transact as a day trader. These are the tools of the trader. A cash account needs to be loaded with cash to facilitate trades. In contrast, a margin account allows for the borrowing of cash from the broker to facilitate trades. Therefore, instead of using their own cash to purchase securities, the trader would take a loan from the broker to facilitate this and pay an interest rate for the service. Both types of accounts have minimum amounts that need to be deposited to be useful to the trader, depending on the broker.

What are the features and services offered by the broker?

Different brokers offer different types of services. A day trader can gain a full-service package from a broker. The broker personally handles the day trader's account and is very hands-on in the service provided. This type of broker service typically comes with higher fees and higher minimum requirements for opening cash and margin accounts. However, it can be of great use to a beginner day trader.

More experienced day traders usually use a discount service that is not as hands-on but has lower fees and minimum account requirements. There are other features to account for when looking into a brokerage service. Consider the speed at which the broker executes trades, the availability of bank wire services, and how trade confirmations are made, to name a few.

Does this broker charge commission fees? If yes, what is the commission fee?

Remember that every broker has their fee structure set up. Be aware of how this affects your bottom dollar before signing up.

CHAPTER SUMMARY

- Brokers are the middleman between traders and the stock market. They are the entities authorized to buy and sell stocks and other securities on the world's stock market and other financial markets.

- The broker is the one who places orders on behalf of day traders for a fee.

- When looking into gaining brokerage representation, a day trader needs to consider whether the broker services are available online. Also, reflect on the broker's reputation, requirements of opening and maintaining broker accounts, features, and fees/charges.

THE 2ND LAW

Aiming for Realistic Profits

CHAPTER 6: LET'S GET STARTED

WHAT DOES DAY TRADING FOR A LIVING LOOK LIKE?

Picture this... You turn on the computer in the morning, and instinct tells you exactly which stocks to invest in to make a million bucks off the bat. *Clickity click click*. With a few strokes of your keyboard, boom, it is done. You have won in every trading bet you made. Your bank account is loaded, and it is not even 10 AM yet. A few minutes later, you drive off in your uber-expensive car, meet up with your super-cool celebrity and Instagram-famous friends, and sip champagne on a rooftop restaurant reserved for members of elite society only... Many people have a similar picture when they think of what a day in the life of a day trader would look like.

That is an excellent fantasy and one that is portrayed all over social media. Sorry to burst your bubble, but that's not what a day trader's life looks like for most of us. There are plenty of day traders making bank, but that's after mastering the art. I've been blessed to make an exceptional living out of it, but it takes hard work. I intend to give you the technical tools to get you started as a day trader and a realistic view of the day-to-day stuff. It ain't glitz and glamor, that's for sure!

Like I mentioned, I've created a cool infographic that really organizes my day and gives you a visual of what a day trader's day looks like. You can find the infographic in this link: bit.ly/Noobsinfographic.

To give you a realistic look at what a day trader's life is like, let me share a sample of what a trading day typically looks like for me. I wake up early to get my morning workout, breakfast, and shower in before 6 AM. Then I get down to work by using the plethora of graphs and other tools to analyze the market to see where I want to bet my money that day. I also have the news running in the background to get a heads up on any significant events that might affect the market. By the time 8 AM rolls around, I am armed and ready to turn my predictions into action. I typically sit at my desk for the next 4 hours and break for lunch. I usually have to order in because I am so terrible in the kitchen.

Once I have eaten, I get back on the ball for about two more hours before throwing in the towel on that trading day. I try to balance my work and personal life (and keep from bouncing off my house walls) by meeting up with friends or family on weekends or engaging in hobbies that I have taken up over the years.

I do not drive an uber-expensive car, even though I can afford to at this stage in my career. I live a comparatively everyday life in the whole scheme of things. I work hard, and I play hard. I am at a comfortable place in my career and do not feel the need or the desire to flash my success. There is nothing wrong with that, mind you, if that is your aspiration. No matter the goals or dreams of the day trader, the trading setup remains the same. Let's jump into that aspect of a day's lifestyle.

TRADING SETUP

Location is one of the most important things to consider as a day trader. You can work from home as I do, or you can choose to lease an office space if you feel that will make you more productive. Make no mistake; you need office space, and this space needs to be comfy! I have a friend who decided it was a good idea to day trade from his couch with his laptop resting on his lap or propped on an old plastic table. Needless to say, he was not happy about the bills he had to deal with when his back and neck needed to be checked out by a chiropractor. We will call him Ted to keep his anonymity in this book. Don't be like Ted.

No matter the location you choose to work from, you need to design an efficient workspace to get the most done in the smallest amount of time. That means designing an efficient workflow as well as having the right equipment for the job. An old laptop running Windows 95 and a dial-up Internet connection will not cut it. Those are bound to crash during your workday. Several times most likely. Those crashes will cost you dearly, so ensure they do not happen by getting the right tools for the job right off the bat.

Your internet connection needs to be reliable and have enough bandwidth to not slow down during your workday. Your computer needs to be top-notch, too. There are no two ways about it. While a laptop will be convenient for checking on your performance while on the go, put together a more elaborate setup for your office space. That includes a computer with a fast processor and plenty of memory. You will also need to have at least two large monitors set up. As a day trader, you'll have your eyes on several things at once, and searching out windows will slow you down significantly. If you are like me, you have a pet peeve about searching out windows, so you can appreciate that this keeps frustration levels down, too. Being able to glance at what you need when you need it will significantly improve your work.

PREPARATION FOR DAY TRADING

As I mentioned earlier, I get up early every morning to prepare for my trading day before the stock market opens. The early bird catches the worm, they say, and I definitely want to catch the worm. You also want to catch the worm too; hence, you read this book and have made it this far.

I aim to get as much recent information as possible. I gather knowledge on stocks and other securities on the market and how the market itself has been trending before determining any trading for that day. Even though I would have had an idea of the direction I wanted to go overnight, so much can happen in the space of a few hours. 2020 is a demonstration of extreme displays of change over a few hours if there ever was one. I do not set anything in stone until about an hour before I start trading for the day.

Graphs and charts are my primary tools of choice for this. These tools provide me with stock and other securities' price histories. You might be asking why I am stuck in the past, but it is a good idea to look back for once. Looking at price history allows me to see patterns in stock and other securities' performance to make predictions about how they will perform in the future. That future performance is what I am betting my trades on. Buying or selling on the stock market is only concerned with the past and the future. Every time you blink, that second's price movement is recorded in the past.

I have three computer monitors set up in my home office. They allow me to monitor many charts and graphs simultaneously. They reveal past information about sectors, niches, particular stocks, and more every time I blink my eyes.

Daily charts and intraday charts are those that I use most frequently during my pre-trading day routine. Daily charts allow me to examine stock and other securities' daily price movements over a defined amount of time, such as a few days, weeks, and months. A daily chart representing a week's worth of data will have 7 data points to represent seven days, and so on. Commonly used daily charts are the line, bar and candlestick charts. Each of these show the closing prices of the security on the days specified.

On the other hand, intraday charts display price movements over intervals that are shorter than a day, such as every 15 minutes. These charts allow for noticing patterns of stock and other securities price behaviors within the space of a day. This is important for a day trader to know since many trades can be opened and closed within a few minutes.

I also utilize weekly charts when I want to find out more extensive information. Line, bar and candlestick charts are also commonly used. They only differ in the time plotted.

Daily, weekly, and intraday charts can be displayed in many formats. Still, most day traders use the candlestick display because of the range of information it shows. We will go more in-depth with the use of candlestick charts in Chapter 13.

Once all the preparations are done, it is time for the exciting bit - placing trade orders.

UNDERSTANDING TRADING ORDERS

After you have done your pre-trading analysis, you will not just place trade orders willy nilly. Many people are under the mistaken assumption that placing a trade order simply means pressing a "buy now" or "sell now" button. Still, the process is more intuitive than that. Of course, there are strategies where you can simply buy or sell stocks and other securities on the trade market. Still, this strategy can become inefficient because you have to continually monitor the performance of the security. Ain't nobody got time for that!

There's the option to use different types of trade orders to give day traders more control. These options include:

Market orders. These orders allow for the purchase or sale of stock or other securities at the current market price. The day trader does not have control over how much they pay to sell or buy that stock. The price is determined by the market. For instance, in the same way that most people are unwilling to pay $5 for a 750ml bottle of water. Particular securities are limited in the price they can be sold for by what traders and investors are willing to pay for them. As such, there is a higher risk of loss in fast-moving markets. Suppose this stock or other securities is being heavily traded. In that case, other orders may be executed ahead of that of the day trader's, which can change the price by the time it is traded. Namely, if a day trader places a market order to purchase 50 shares of stock at $40 per share, by the time the deal is done, the price may have risen to $42. This change may be because that stock is wanted by many investors. The price increased to show that increase in demand.

Limit orders. Imagine a trader wants to purchase shares of stock for no more than $25 per share. The limit order ensures that the transaction does not take place unless that criteria is met. These orders allow for the purchase or sale of stock and other securities at a specific price. It can be referred to as a buying limit order or sell limit order; this depends on whether a stock or other security is being bought or sold. This type of order allows a day trader to buy or sell at the price they prefer, so the price is not controlled by the market.

This command specifies that the buyer will not pay more than a specific price for a stock share regarding a buy limit order. That specific price is the limit order. Another example, suppose a day trader is considering buying stock, which is currently priced at $15. In that case, they can set a limit order to purchase 100 shares of that stock if the price goes down to $10 per share. The transaction will be facilitated automatically if this criterion is met. The trade will only be executed if those 100 shares of stock decrease to $10 per share.

In the case of a sell limit order, it specifies that a day trader will not sell a stock share under a specific price, which places that price as the limit. Suppose the seller is considering selling stock, which is currently priced at $15 a share. In that case, they can place a sell limit order at $18 and only sell the stock shares if the stock's value increases. With the increase, the order will be executed.

Stop order. Which can be referred to as a stop-loss order. This order is used to minimize losses associated with day trading by initiating a command to sell a stock when it reaches a specific price. Let's illustrate this with an example whereby the day trader is considering selling stock when it's at $13. If its value declines to $10, the stop order would be placed at that mark. The command will be executed automatically.

Stop limit order. This is a hybrid form that combines a stop order and a limit order. Therefore, it requires that the day trader place two different prices: stop price and limit price. When the stock price becomes the stop price, then the order becomes a limit order. Stop Limit Order is one of those things where you understand once you become experienced with it. For now, here's an example. Say a day trader owns stock with a value of $50 and would like to sell it if the price dips below $45. But only if the stock can be sold for $43 or more. Accordingly, the day trader will set a stop limit order by creating a stop price of $50 and a limit price of $43. When the stock decreases to $45, the limit of that trade becomes $43.

Trailing stop order. This type of trade order is similar to a stop order. Still, instead of being controlled by market price, the trade order is based on the percentage by which the security changes market price. By way of illustration, a day trader can initiate a trailing stop order for 10% after purchasing a stock for $15. If the stock price decreases by 10% or more, then the stop order will come into effect. On a side note, the 10% decrease totals $1.50. So, the order will automatically go into effect when the stock price reaches $13.50.

CHAPTER SUMMARY

- A look into the realistic day in a day trader's life starts with prep work to determine the best strategies for investing before the markets open. This prep work entails analyzing graphs and charts such as daily, weekly, and intraday charts to determine patterns in price movement of stocks and other securities.

- Once the day trader has made predictions about stocks' future price movement based on historical data, they can execute trade orders to profit.

- Day traders use trade order to have more control over how trades are executed. Common types of trade orders include market orders, limit orders, stop orders, stop-limit orders, and trailing stop orders.

Chapter 7: Risk and Account Management Plus Day Trading Strategy & Analysis

Being as profitable as can be as a day trader leans as heavily towards taking the smallest possible losses as it does to making as much money as possible. Keeping your losses down to a minimum relies on managing risk well, which we will focus on in this chapter.

Risk Management and Account Management

I have mentioned risk management several times in the course of this book, and at this point, you might be tired of hearing it. I get that. There are no horses or magic potions or superheroes in this story, though when you think about it, all of those things would require some risk management, too. But I digress. The stress placed on risk management in the world of day trading is because of the significant impact it could have on your career. You might have a winning streak and gain thousands in profits only to lose it all with just one or two poorly planned trades. Do not skimp on the risk management process of planning your day trading career, as these might just be the strategies that help keep on building your bank account.

MONEY MANAGEMENT

Let's start managing risks by managing your money. Money is the backbone of day trading—of all the financial markets of the world. (Thank you, Captain Obvious). Therefore, ensure that your money is managed correctly. Managing your money means knowing how it flows in and out of your accounts. These are not processes that should happen spontaneously. You need to have iron-clad control over this if you do not want to struggle at not only day trading but at life. Tips for managing your money effectively as a day trader include:

- Defining your short-term and long-term money goals.

- Creating an accounting and filing system to stay organized and efficiently track the flow of money in and out of your accounts.

- Never investing or spending money that you cannot afford to lose.

- Ensuring that your money is spread across a diverse portfolio.

- Ensuring that you manage the amounts that you bet on trades. The best strategy for doing this is discussed next.

THE ONE-PERCENT ACCOUNT MANAGEMENT RULE

This is one of the first risk management rules that all traders learn. This is a highly effective rule, yet it is a simple one. It states that a trader should never risk more than 1% of their account value while participating in a single trade. Let's assume if your account has a value of $50,000, you should never stake more than $500—which is 1% of $50,000—on trading any type of security. This rule is so effective because you cannot lose more than 1% of your account value in a single trade if the trade does not work out in your favor. This rule protects you because no trader wins in every trade. You will definitely experience loss, and with the 1% rule on your side, you will never be more than 1% poorer because of it.

MARKET ORDERS

Using the one-percent strategy is not as simple as trading only 1% of your account per trade. It gets a little more complicated when you actually practice it. When you risk this 1% of your account, you stand to make a higher percentage return on your investment. This makes sense even if the price movement on the market is minimal.

Meaning, while day traders typically shoot for a return like 2% or 3% on a single trade, you can make a 5% return because of a simple price movement in a short space of time.

The key to achieving this is to set targets or goals for your trades. If you are lucky, you will reach that target. If you're blessed, you can achieve more than you set out to. However, you can't ride this train of luck forever; you will eventually hit a wall. As a day trader, holding onto a trade too long not only risks the profit that you have made but also threatens your investment if the train derails. That is the nature of the financial markets, especially when day traders are placing bets on volatility. Accordingly, you will want to limit the amount that you stand to lose in a single trade and so have an exit strategy in place for when trades are not working out in your favor.

This is where stop-loss orders and take-profit points come in. A take-profit point is a limit order that indicates a trader will exit a trade while retaining a profit. This order does not go into effect unless the price of the security reaches that limit. By way of illustration, suppose a trader shoots for making a 3% profit on a trade but has a take-profit limit of 5%. In that case, he will not exit until that 5% limit is reached, even if he has already seen the trade being beneficial at a 3% return.

This type of market order is usually used together with a stop-loss order. A stop-loss order is the opposite of a take-profit point. It indicates at what loss percentage a trader will back out of a trade. The stop-loss order will go into effect if the security moves in a direction that does not benefit the trader.

Both of these market orders are great for risk management in the short term as they allow for the fast in-and-out movement of trades. Day traders make these points of determination by performing technical analyses.

DAY TRADING STRATEGY AND ANALYSIS

Technical analysis refers to how a day trader examines the financial market they have chosen to invest in to determine their next moves. This examination identifies the market's strengths and weaknesses at the current time to use those conditions to profit. Several tools can be used in that effort. Let's take a look at some of the more popular tools for analyzing the stock market and other financial markets for trading options.

Check out my magazine if you'd like more on building better strategies and investing tips. This is the one I recommended earlier. You can find it here: bit.ly/NoobsMagazine.

CHART PATTERN ANALYSIS

Price charts are one of the most essential tools for analyzing the financial markets. These charts depict price movement over a specific time. Following this movement allows day traders to notice trends that can be capitalized on. A few common types of price charts include the line chart and open-high-low-close chart.

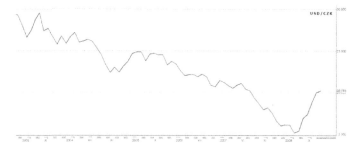

7-1. Image of line chart.

As the name suggests, line charts use one line to show price movement over the specified amount of time. Data points are placed along that single line, so the line moves up and down. This type of chart is easy to interpret, and thus, this is one of the first types of charts that day traders learn to use. However, this chart's simplicity does not indicate other factors that need to be factored into day traders' consideration.

90

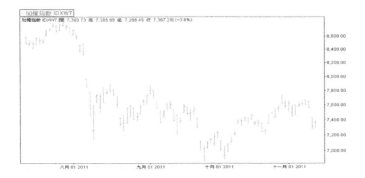

7-2. Image of open-high-low-close price chart.

On the other hand, the open-high-low-close price chart is more complex. It shows price movement from the highest to the lowest points over a specific period. Time is typically a smaller unit, like one hour or one day, compared to line charts, which typically indicate price movement over weeks, months, and years.

SUPPORT AND RESISTANCE LEVELS

Support is the point at which the price of a security stops declining. Resistance is the opposite: it is the point where the price of a security stops rising. These prices are used in tandem with analyzing price charts. You will typically notice the support and resistance levels highlighted with angled or horizontal lines on price charts. These are called trendlines.

Trendlines allow the day trader to visualize how the financial market is currently moving and what it is likely to do in the future. It is essential to know support and resistance levels because it allows the trader to decide how to enter a trading position. Typically, a day trader will enter a trade position by buying long when the security price moves above the resistance level. On the other hand, a day trader will likely enter a trade by selling short if the price of the security breaks above the support level. So, buy long above resistance and sell low above support. For a beginner, I don't recommend shorting (or selling short). It's risky and requires lots of experience.

CHAPTER SUMMARY

- Risk management is the process of planning your day trading career to minimize losses.

- Money management is necessary for risk management. Managing your money means knowing how money flows in and out of your accounts.

- The one-percent rule is another risk management tactic. It states that a trader should never risk more than 1% of their account value to make a single trade.

- Stop-loss orders and take-profit points are market orders that help with risk management.

- To find the best stock to trade, day traders need to know chart pattern analysis and support and resistance levels.

THE 3RD LAW

Bringing it Together

Chapter 8: Trading Psychology

If every Tom, Dick, and Harry could be a day trader, then the career would be oversaturated. The fact is that becoming a day trader is not for everyone (becoming a successful one, that is). To find success as a day trader, you need to be oriented in a certain way mentally to get the job done right. Let's talk about the psychological traits a trader needs to have to be profitable.

There's a lot of things to consider when day trading, and I've creating a magazine that covers a few of them. I cover some super important stuff like how to *how to pick profitable stocks* to *trading strategy*. This is my magazine I was talking about earlier in the book. Visit here to download: <u>bit.ly/NoobsMagazine</u>. I highly recommend it!

Successful Day Trading Psychology

Even if you know and understand all the essential skills to be a day trader, it all amounts to nothing if you do not have a day trader's mindset. It would be like entering a car race with a bicycle and expecting to cross the finish line first. Getting your mental wavelength aligned with a day trader is extremely important. That wavelength consists of thinking quickly on your feet, being self-disciplined, and controlling your emotions.

Let's start by talking about the importance of managing your emotions first. Excitement and anticipation can go a long way in fueling your drive on this day trading highway. It's when day traders are motivated by greed or fear that the wheels start coming loose.

On the next point of developing an effectual mindset for day trading—which is being able to roll with the punches and make quick decisions—there needs to be a balance. Of course, there are times when you need to enter and exit trades at the snap of a finger. That requires you to have the presence of mind to weigh the pros and cons of those trades. The point that negatively tips the scales is when day traders make snap decisions that are not backed by logic or experience but by emotions. You have to control your emotions when you make trades, or sooner or later, you will get the short end of the stick. Many day traders, even experienced ones, sometimes deal with fear. Their fear may stem from losing out on a trade or other factors, but the fear always means that the day trader reacts to something that threatens their position. That threat is typically directed at the potential profit that he or she will earn. Effective risk management is the only way to get past this natural emotional response. Most of the time, the fear that we feel in any aspect of life is overblown. Effective risk management helps you see the true magnitude of the things that you fear.

Greed is a troubling condition when it comes to day trading. "Pigs get slaughtered." That is a Wall Street saying that addresses the scenario of traders and investors trying to play out positions for too long to gain more. This tactic usually backfires.

The truth is that many people get into day trading to make a quick buck. Or, they believe that day trading is an enchanted pathway to great wealth. Of course, there is occasionally the case of someone hitting gold right out of the gate with day trading, but that is not the norm. Therefore, being greedy and making trades based on disillusion will only lead to catastrophe. Greed is a natural inclination to get more, and it is difficult to overcome in most cases. Still, it can be done with rational thinking and working based on an effective trading plan.

Controlling your emotions and making decisions that work for you instead of against you all comes down to self-discipline. You can only be a great day trader if you set a path for yourself and stay on it despite the obstacles. Things are not always going to go your way (welcome to this thing called life), and you have to know how to remain firm instead of being swayed by the current swing of things. A great way to be more self-disciplined in your day trading is by setting up rules for yourself about operating your trading business. That leads me to discuss our next day trading essential, which is creating a day trading plan.

Connect with other day traders in our community for support and knowledge. We learn faster when we all collaborate and connect. It would be great to have you. Join here: bit.ly/NoobsTradingFacebook.

PSYCHOLOGICAL AND TECHNICAL ASPECTS OF DETERMINING WHICH STOCK TO BUY

Developing a trading plan is the first thing you need to do when you commit to this career. This will list your motivation for starting and sticking with this field. You also should look at the resources available to you. Plan how you'll build on your resources, define your daily trading approach, set goals, and so much more. Having no trading plan is a common sign that greed is a day trader's motivation because it shows that the trader did not sit down to do his or her homework.

Having a trading plan ensures that you do not act on your emotions while you are day trading. As part of ensuring that you make the maximum profit possible, have a road map guiding you. Your trading plan serves as your guide.

Therefore, before you start trading, or even paper trading (which means practicing without real money), you need to sit down and determine:

- What your long-term and short-term goals are

- How much money you will be able to invest in day trading

- How much time you will be able to commit to day trading and whether it will be every day

- What type of securities you would like to trade

- What strategies you will use to find opportunities in the stock market

- How much you are willing to risk with every trade, and what determines that risk

- Your rules for risk management

- What strategy you will use to ensure that losses are minimal

- What strategies you will use to figure out which stocks and other securities are worthy of your investment

These are only a few of the determinations that need to be made when creating a trading plan. A lot goes into creating an effective trading plan, which is typically not done in one sitting. Just like creating a business plan, you need to keep your emotions out of the process and allow your logical brain to guide you. Once you have formularized this plan and it is sound, this is a tool that will enable you to grow and progress in the long-term and the short-term. One of the best things about an effective trading plan is that it summarizes your psychology. Let's face it, there are times when we all slip up. The brain is a fickle thing, prone to changing directions in thought quickly. Brains. Can't live with them, can't live without them, am I right? Luckily, having a trading plan allows you to rely on rationality and reasoning rather than your mind's whims.

The trading plan also allows you to notice what works for you as a day trader and what does not. It sets up the precedent for you to notice trends in your actions and build on the most profitable actions for you. Your trading plan is fluid and can be changed at any time. I highly encourage you to set up a schedule for regularly updating your trading plan weekly or monthly to incorporate new ideas and eliminate bad ones. That will help you stay on course with what you have envisioned for yourself and your trading career.

The last thing I would like to mention when creating a trading plan is this: do not limit yourself. Allow yourself to dream big. Realize that the sky's the limit with trading, even though it takes work to build the career you desire. The power of dreaming big is that flooding your brain with images of you succeeding allows you to be better positioned to manifest those visions. Do not limit yourself to thinking that you can make just a few hundred dollars a month by day trading. Many day traders make hundreds of thousands and millions of dollars every year day trading. Nothing is stopping you from accomplishing the same thing except you and your psychological approach to this career.

CHAPTER SUMMARY

- A practical day trader needs to be decisive, self-disciplined, and control his or her emotions.

- Along with developing the right psychology, a day trader needs to create a trading plan.

- A trading plan highlights a day trader's goals, plans, and strategies.

CHAPTER 9: IMPLEMENTING A SUCCESSFUL TRADE STEP BY STEP

You have many tools that help you successfully get started and perform a day trade. Ensure that you have it all solidified in your mind. Here is a demonstration of how I go about performing a simple day trade. It is not magic and potions. It is not complicated. It's about following a reliable system that works.

CREATING A WATCH LIST

My trading plan starts with knowing what stocks that I want to trade. This leads me to develop a watch list to manage prospective stocks for investment. Creating a watch list also allows me to plan ahead and be prepared when tradable stocks enter the arena. Before I move forward, I want you to understand the difference between a portfolio and a watch list. Some beginner day traders get the two confused, but we will set you up to not have that confusion. A portfolio is a list of the stocks and other securities you own (as a day trader). A watch list can display both the securities you own and others you have selected. It can include securities that you've shown interest in but do not own.

You do not have to get fancy when creating a watch list. In fact, I advise against it. So, without further ado, here is a breakdown of how I create watch lists:

- Keep everything simple to clear up any cobwebs that may develop from over-complication.

- Ensure that you develop a schedule for combing through a watch list so that you can spot stocks of interest that become tradable at the earliest opportunity.

- Ensure that your watch list has at least 16 items that you can peruse daily.

- You develop a watch list by having criteria for what you look for in tradable stock and other securities. Start off broad with these criteria and then narrow them down. An excellent strategy for having this criterion is to pick stocks that are popular and already performing well. They are likely to be high in volume as they are of interest to buyers and sellers.

- You do not have to limit yourself to one watch list and create multiple watch lists of different fit criteria.

- A few rules for creating a watchlist are based on the criteria for riding trends on the stock market. These signals indicate potential unusual trends that can be capitalized on, and noticing higher than usual trading volume.

- To create valuable criteria that will allow you to be as profitable as possible. Continuously analyze the stock market, the industries you are interested in trading in, and the changing levels of capitalization in the companies interested in those industries.

Like everything else in the day trading game, experiment and fine-tune the strategies outlined above to suit you and your trading style. The more you familiarize yourself with creating watch lists and analyzing stocks and other securities for trading, the more comfortable you will become with the practice.

PLANNING THE TRADE (ENTRY, EXIT, AND STOP LOSS)

After you have identified the stocks you want to trade based on your watch list, you needed to develop a trading plan before jumping in headfirst. Here is a quick breakdown of how to do this:

- When developing your trading plan, you need to consider that the market will not always work with you. Respect the fact that the stock market may work against your predictions and expectations. Therefore, you needed to have exit and entry points backed by stop-loss orders so that your risks are mitigated to a minimum. We'll touch more on what exit and entry points are later in the book.

- Next, develop a strategy for entering the trade. To enter the trade, use indicators such as support and resistance levels. The use of trend lines also allows you to jump in at the right time. Jumping the gun too early is a sure way to make losses. Be patient and allow your analytical and scanning tools to do the work for you.

- Setting a target price comes next. After your entry point has been determined, you need to set a target price. You want a clear picture of where you are starting and the profit opportunity you are chasing with the trade.

- Next comes the implementation of a stop-loss order to protect your investment and manage risks. This is where you use a percentage or a dollar amount to do this. Remember that trailing stops can also be implemented for further protection. You'll see me cover this later.

CARRYING OUT THE PLAN

Here is a simple sample of the execution of a trading plan. It takes into account multiple trades simultaneously because, as a day trader, you will be making multiple trades. You cannot hope to make a substantial profit-making one trade at a time.

- How many trades will I use to measure my trading performance daily? *10*

- What time of day will I enter new trading positions? *9:45 AM–10:20 AM EST time*

- By what time of day do I expect to close all open positions? *12:30 PM EST time*

- How much will I risk per trade? *1.5% of the position*

- What is my exit strategy? *When the stock crosses below the 10-period SMA (simple moving average) on 5 minutes.* An SMA is the average of a selected range of prices, such as the closing prices. Namely, the closing price of a stock for 3 days may have been 15, 16, and 14, so the SMA is 15.

- What are my trading criteria? *High volume, early opening range breakouts, tight spreads, and consolidation before the breakout*

CHAPTER SUMMARY

- A simple execution of a day trade starts typically with the development of a watch list. There are a few rules for creating useful watch lists. Keep it simple, have a schedule for studying the watch lists. Start broad, narrow the criteria you are looking for within securities, and create multiple watch lists based on different criteria.

- Once the securities on your watch list become available for trading, develop a trading plan to support those transactions with entry points, target prices, and exit strategies.

THE 4TH LAW

Stick to the Plan

CHAPTER 10: PLATFORMS AND TOOLS TO KEEP YOU SHARP

It sounds exciting to scroll across several screens for several hours with an intense look in your eyes and a burning desire to find a perfect stock to trade daily. Doesn't it? Sure, the imagery sounds good and well, but I can tell you that it gets tiresome real fast from experience. That intense look of concentration can turn into a crazed one as you pull out your hair in frustration. This is where stock scanners can step in to prevent you from having to spend 3 to 4 hours every morning scanning for suitable stock to trade daily... They allow you to keep your luscious locks on your head and a healthy look in your eye. The action that can take hours can be done in minutes with stock scanners. This chapter focuses on the magnificent tools and how you can use it to your advantage as a day trader.

WHAT ARE STOCK SCANNING TOOLS

10-1. Image of stock scanning tool in action

A stock scanner is a type of software that generates hundreds and thousands of stock listings almost instantly to fit the criteria that have been inputted into the software search. You can enter "high average trading volume" into the search bar as a case in point. With the click of a mouse, you can have every stock that meets the criteria that you have set without having to flick through several screens for hours on end. The benefits that make stock scanners invaluable to day traders are saving time, money, energy, and hair strands. This software allows you to place your focus where it really counts. To look for more trading opportunities so that you can make as much profit in as little time as possible.

As a day trader, you will eventually encounter the term stock screeners. Many traders mistakenly use stock screeners and the stock scanners interchangeably, but there is a difference. Stock screeners came about as a product of the infancy stage of the World Wide Web development and are websites where a trader can log in and scan stocks using essential criteria. FinViz is one such example. It makes market information easily accessible to traders and investors. While they do the job, stop screeners are not as advanced or useful for long-term day trading as stock scanners. Stock scanners have been developed and advanced as the reach of the Internet expands. Stock scanners allow you to have the information you need in real-time to see every trading opportunity as it comes. For example, as soon as a price change occurs on the stock market, this tool will reflect this. These tools allow day traders to be the early bird that catches the worm.

FINDING SCANNING TOOLS

Like any other piece of software on the market, there are several varieties to choose from, and the same truth holds true for stock scanners. Stock scanners have been developed to meet the technological needs of the stock market access requirements, trading style, and trading strategies to suit day traders. Some stock scanners run from your browser, while others can be loaded from your operating system. Some software allows you to access the financial market by paying a flat monthly fee. In contrast, others allow you to pay thousands of dollars upfront to own the software outright. The differences between stock scanners are way too numerous to mention. Still, this section is dedicated to breaking down stock scanners by types to better understand what is out there and what will work best for you.

TECHNICAL STOCK SCANNERS

This type of stock scanner uses technical analysis criteria such as the movement of prices, technical indicators, trading volume, and chart patterns to pull up a list of tradeable stock for the day trader. Amongst others, the trader may search for stocks with a trading volume of 1000 or more, and the stock scanner will pull up these results.

FUNDAMENTAL STOCK SCANNERS

This type of stock scanner uses fundamental analysis as its base. It focuses on fundamental criteria, as the name suggests. The fundamental analysis describes the company's information that has the stock up for trading's performance. That was a mouth full. It relates to commercial activity, profit margin, earnings per share, and returns on equity, to name a few items that need to be considered as the trader deliberates on their company's stocks. As an illustration, a stock scanner providing that a company made a $350,000 profit last year is an example of fundamental analysis. To use this type of stock scanner, you may input the criteria such as earnings per share. Once that list has popped up on your screen, you can do more in-depth research on the particular stocks that you are deliberating trading.

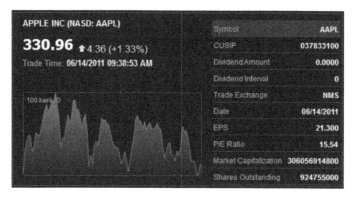

10-2. Image of stock scanner displaying specific criteria stated.

POST-MARKET STOCK SCANNERS

This type of stock scanner monitors stock activity outside of typical trading hours, hence the name post-market analysis. The stock activity does not come to a standstill because the stock market has closed. Therefore, there is a lot of data available to analyze outside the stock market's operating hours that might affect stock behavior during operating trading hours.

INTRADAY STOCK SCANNERS

This type of stock scanner contrasts with the post-market stock scanner and pulls up stock information based on criteria that use real-time action on the stock market while operating. An example is StockFetcher. Based on its text-based filtering, you can use plain-English phrases to build your custom stock screens. This type of stock scanners is highly robust because there is a lot of information that needs to be relayed quickly. If you are a day trader that likes to be on the ball or in the thick of things all the time, this is the best stock scanner for you as it allows you to see market trends as they are happening.

The stocks scanner or scanners you choose are largely dependent on your user's trading style and strategies. Yet, another reason why it pays to start this process with a sound plan.

HOW DO SCANNING TOOLS WORK?

The intricacies of how a stock scanner works depend on the type you use and the particular software chosen. No matter the type of stock scanner you choose, ensure that you spend the time necessary to learn its ins and outs to gain your money's worth.

Still, I will provide a few things that will help you out across the board. The first tip is to set up intraday alerts.

This ensures that you know an unusual movement on the stock market even if you are not an intraday trader. This will allow you to catch market trends early to use any opportunities that arise.

The next step is to develop watch lists. Constantly checking for new stocks to trade every single day is inefficient. It is more productive to establish watch lists that allow you to monitor collections of stocks in sectors and markets that you find interesting to quickly locate them easily and understand how they are performing with a quick glance. The beauty of this strategy is that you can create several watch lists at a time. Like those made to keep an eye on what sectors are of interest to you and others. And to keep an eye on stocks that are frequently traded. For example, a trader may keep a watch list of stocks with a trading volume of 2000 or more. Trading volume refers to the total number of shares that were trading during a given period.

WHAT CAN YOU DO WITH SCANNING TOOLS?

Now as good as scanning tools are, there is one limitation: the day trader. Stock scanners are only as good as you use them. Therefore, you need to have a structured scanning strategy to find the most favorable stocks to day trade easier. The way to make the software work best for you is to customize it. You use the features available to see stock listing as you prefer and suit your trading strategy. This will show you only stocks within the parameters like volume, resistance, and price relevant to your trading method.

If you allow it to, you will become overwhelmed by the sheer amount of information provided by stock scanners. You have to learn to see past the dust to find the information that pertains to you and your strategy when it comes to day trading stock. You must know the features available through your scanning tool to allow the popup of information that makes your job as a day trader most convenient and most profitable. This information is provided by the company that produced the scanning tool. This is why it is essential to be familiar with the features offered by that tool.

CHAPTER SUMMARY

- A stock scanner is a type of software that generates results of hundreds and thousands of stock listings almost instantly to fit the criteria that have been inputted into the software search.

- Stock scanners come in several different types. The main types are technical analysis stock scanners, fundamental analysis stock scanners, post-market stock scanners, and intraday stock scanners.

- Different stock scanners work in different manners to provide different types of information. The stock scanner that a day trader uses is dependent on his or her needs and strategies as a day trader.

CHAPTER 11: ASSESS A COMPANY'S STOCK

Stocks are a typical investment in the stock market… Duh! Hence, they are a typical investment for day traders. Hence, you cannot just go about buying and selling stock like they are the fruit you find on the ground. These fruits were attached to a tree. That analogy applies to stock. Think of stocks as the fruit, and they come from trees, which is the company that produces these stocks.

When buying and trading stocks as a day trader, you must carefully consider the company that has listed these stocks. Like a poisoned tree will likely produce low-quality and undesirable fruits, a malfunctioning or corrupt company will likely not have desirable stock. But you will not know that if you did not take the time to do your research. As a day trader, familiarize yourself with the companies that list the stocks you are interested in trading. That will save you from biting into a lot of bruised apples!

I touch on things like *how to find profitable stock* and *how to value companies* in my magazine. You can find it for free here: bit.ly/NoobsMagazine, courtesy of me.

TAKING A COMPANY'S INDUSTRY INTO ACCOUNT

The industry in which a company operates influences the price that's demanded with its stock. To break it down simply... not all industries are created equal. That is to say, companies that operate in the energy industry can demand higher prices for stocks than those operating in consumer staples, even though this is a modern industry. Apart from the energy industry, some of the other industries that can demand a high price for stocks include healthcare, financial, communications, information technology, real estate, and utilities. No matter the industry you choose to invest in, it is crucial to diversify your portfolio even as a day trader. Do not just stick to one industry.

However, you cannot just act like a toddler and dive into the pool's deep end. Consider the different industries from different vantages before you make your choices as each one operates differently. For instance, even though energy is a heavyweight contender in stock trading, it is still susceptible to downward price movements. It's due to significant events like political playouts and natural disasters. You need to consider the factors that affect the industries that you choose to invest in. Just because the industry has a good day or period doesn't mean that you will indefinitely benefit. Primarily if the company whose stock you are interested in trading does not operate smoothly.

DETERMINING A COMPANY'S FINANCIAL STABILITY

Of course, how a company is doing financially is an indicator of how well you can expect its stock to perform on the stock market. Its financial information can allow you to notice if it is borrowing more money than its sales incur. And how it's stacking up against other companies in the industry, etc.

The company's financial statements, particularly its balance sheet, are an excellent tool for examining how stable its finances are. The balance sheet provides an overview of its assets (stuff that it owns) about its liabilities (stuff that it owes).

Looking at a company's ratio is also a great way of determining its financial stability. A few of the different ratios that you can consider:

- **Liquidity ratios**. This is a measure of how much cash and other easily liquid assets a company has to cover its debts. If the current ratio is below 1, the company is in financial trouble and cannot pay off its debts.

- **Efficiency ratios**. This measure typically spans a three to five-year period. It allows insight into a company's cash flow and the results of its operations and is a percentage figure. An efficiency ratio of 50% or lower means that a company's revenue is increasing.

- **Profitability ratios**. This measure compares how a company is performing concerning other ones within an industry. It is often used to evaluate a company's financial viability. If a company has a profit margin of 35%, it has earned a $0.35 profit on every dollar earned in sales.

- **Leverage ratios**. This is a measure of a company's debt compared to its asset in the long run. This is an excellent indicator of how capable a company is of repaying its debts or how capable it is of taking additional debts to support new opportunities that arise. Let's say, if a company has total liabilities of $300,000 and total equity of $250,000, this leverage ratio is 1.2. A leverage ratio of less than 1 is ideal. Still, many profitable companies have a higher ratio due to expansion and growth.

Check out my piece on how to use annual reports to choose the right companies. You can find it in my magazine that I recommended earlier: bit.ly/NoobsMagazine.

LOOKING BACK AT HISTORICAL EARNINGS AND SALES GROWTH

To comfortably assess a stock's future, a day trader needs to assess its historical earnings to cast his future revenue and growth projections. There is a great wealth of knowledge to be discovered from looking in the past. That knowledge comes with wealth that can nicely pad a day trader's bank account when looking at a company's financial history.

Many things affect stock. For instance, a company's revenue generated in the past and forecasted to generate in the future. Suppose a company is forecasted to have a high rate of growth in the upcoming periods. In that event, its stock will gain a higher value on the stock market than other competitors in that same industry. This will gain a buyer's interest and further drive up the stock price. The opposite is true, as well. Suppose a company has not performed financially significant in the past or forecasted to not perform financially well in the future. In that case, these facts will negatively affect its stock value. Buyer interest is likely to be low and so further negatively impact the price of the stock.

Making trades based on the predictions on a company's future earnings needs to be approached with care. Making decisions on trades based on unreliable or inaccurate sources will only lead you down a dark tunnel of loss and despair. I say this not to be overdramatic, even though I do love a good drama. Instead, I say this to imprint your day trades' consequences if you use wrong sources to make trade decisions.

The most reliable and accurate way to know what is forecasted for a company's financial future is to look at what financial analysts say. Financial analysts work for and with financial institutions. They do this by keeping an ear to the ground to gain information about companies, their actual financial performance, and how this will likely impact their financial future.

Luckily, you do not have to pay vast sums of money to gain financial analysts' advice to learn the expected future growth or decline in a company's value. The Internet makes it easy for you, as it does so many other things. Websites like Yahoo Finance, allow you to look up financial information about specific companies, such as the expected earnings per year.

Still, you need to take the information that you receive with a grain of salt. It has been noticed that many financial analysts err on an optimistic side when making predictions about the growth of a company's earnings. That is not to say that their predictions are wrong, only that they can be predictions that are higher than realistic. For example, suppose financial analysts say that a company is predicted to have 15% earnings growth. In that case, this will more likely pan out to be closer to 6% growth. Therefore, you will need to be cautious when using financial analyst information and make contingency plans if that information does not work.

Luckily, that is not the only way you can bank off a company's potential future earnings. Historical earning per share (EPS) growth can also give you indicators. Historical EPS growth gives you a mirror to look back on the company's earnings over the last decade. Again, this is something that you still need to keep your thinker's hat on for. Even if a company might have had a high growth rate over the last ten years, is it reasonable to expect to keep up that growth rate in the coming decade? While a company can grow well over the coming decade, this rate will likely not be as fast or high. Consider that the growth rate is likely not going to be as high, and adjust your trades accordingly.

Other company revenue information that you should account for when making trades include return on equity. Which means determining what was invested in a company by investors and owners. You should also account for the rate at which a company can sustain its growth without taking on more debts. Finally, you need to view a company's growth rate from a realistic one, not one where a company is growing at a maximum rate. Always account for the things that can go wrong and protect your profits.

CHECKING OUT THE COMPETITION

Many people get leery when they hear the term competition when it comes to business. Still, competition is a great sign, as it is an indicator that the industry is profitable. It also forces companies to be innovative to keep their current customers and clients, boosting their efforts to attract new customers and clients. This means greater profits and, thus, the increased value of the stock.

Competition can come in two different forms. The first form is known as direct competition. This refers to other companies that sell the same products or services to the same clientele or customer base. The second type of competition is known as indirect competition. This refers to other companies that do not sell the same product or offer the same services as others but compete digitally. This can potentially pull customers' and clients' attention away.

It is essential to evaluate a company's competition. Doing so gives an overview of how it's performing compared to other businesses in that industry. Also, it provides a gauge of how that company's stock is performing in contrast to other ones.

Ways in which you can identify the direct competitors include conducting market research and looking into customer feedback. Those are ways you can analyze the indirect competition. This includes doing keyword research and analyzing search engines for results for keywords that a company identifies with.

CONSIDERING A COMPANY'S VALUE

A company's market value represents its stock price, which is multiplied by the outstanding shares. Market value is also known as its market capitalization or market cap.

Think about it like this: company stock price x outstanding shares = market cap.

A company's stock price is proportional to its value. It represents the scented changes in markets was at any given time. An example of this is a company with 20 million shares, with each share worth $100. This would give the company a market capitalization of $2 billion. Companies can be classified as large-cap companies, midcap companies, and small-cap companies.

Large-cap companies typically have a market value of at least $10 billion. This is because they have a reputation for producing high-quality goods and services, steady growth, and a history whereby they are consistently providing dividend payments to investors. Think of large-cap companies as the dominant players in well-established industries. This translates into them having higher price stocks that are typically safer to invest in.

Mid-cap companies have a market value that ranges between $2 billion and $10 billion. Such companies are well established within the industries and are experiencing rapid growth or are expected to experience rapid growth. Such companies are still in the process of improving their overall competitiveness and are gaining increasing market shares. Therefore, this translates into the value of such companies' stock rising in value and usually being a safe bet for stock market traders.

Small-cap companies typically have a market value of between $300 million and $2 billion. Such companies are typically just emerging in established markets or are showing potential in emerging industries. These companies are the riskiest to invest in because they are vulnerable to competition from more established companies and industries. However, a day trader might find immense profit; thus, companies have a significant potential for growth and, therefore, for sharply increased stock prices.

CHAPTER SUMMARY

- When considering a stock for trading, a day trader also needs to consider the company listing that stock. The source can determine how well that stock trades and how much a day trader profits from trading it.

- The industry in which a company operates plays a big part in the price to demand its stock. Some industries are more profitable when it comes to other trading stock wisely.

- A company's financial stability is also an indicator of how well you can expect its stock to perform on the stock market. Looking at a company's financial statements like the balance sheet gives you an excellent base for gauging its financial performance. Its ratios, such as liquidity ratio, efficiency ratio, profitability ratio, and leverage ratio, are excellent financial stability indicators.

- A company's historical earnings and growth expectations also need to be considered when looking at a stock's profit potential when day trading. A day trader needs to assess its historical earnings to cast his future revenue and growth projections. Financial analysts can provide reliable information to determine sales growth, but this is not perfect. Day traders also have the option of historical earning per share (EPS) growth. That's the return on equity that was invested in a company by investors and owners. It's the rate at which a company can sustain its growth without taking on more debt. It's done to gain a realistic view of a company's growth potential whose stock they consider trading.

- Competition forces companies to be innovative to keep their current customers and clients while attracting new customers and clients. This means greater profits and, thus, the increased value of the stock. Competition comes in direct and indirect forms. Direct competition refers to other companies that sell the same products or services to the same clientele or customer base as a company. Indirect competition refers to other companies that do not sell the same product or offer the same services as a company but compete with the company digitally, pulling attention away. Doing market research, looking into customer feedback, doing keyword research, and analyzing search engines identify the direct and indirect competition that a company has.

- Its market value, also known as its market capitalization or market cap, represents its stock price multiplied by its outstanding shares. Companies can be classified in three ways. Large-cap has a market value of at least $10 billion. Mid-cap has a market value that ranges between $2 billion and $10 billion. And, Small-cap has a market value of between $300 million and $2 billion. These types of market capitalization come with risks and rewards. It is up to the day trader to determine which market capitalization to trade into, which best suits their interests.

CHAPTER 12: HOW TO FIND THOSE STOCKS

TRADABLE STOCKS IN PLAY

After locating the companies that you would like to invest in, you cannot just go about investing in those stocks with a method of *eeny, meeny, miny, moe*. The fact is that most company's stock is relatively constant in nature and move very slow in either direction. They only shift in value in extreme ways to allow traders to make big profits when they produce negative or positive trading actions. This only typically happens a couple of times per year. Long-term investors are more likely to make profits from this slow movement over time.

This leaves quite the dilemma, doesn't it? How do you trade stocks in profitable industries and companies if their stocks are not volatile? The answer is that you target your search for tradeable stock, and that focus needs to be on stocks in play. Stocks are in play when they belong to a company purchased by another entity like another company or individual. This is called a takeover target. Let's look at an example…

Let's call our company Staple Brite, and (you guessed it) the company sells staples. The company does exceptionally well, and its balance sheet shows that it is rapidly acquiring cash and other assets. This puts the company in an advantageous position. So, investors have been putting on the pressure to sell the company for months. Staple Brite heads begin to yield to the pressure, and they make the decision to sell. It then announces that it is exploring partnerships with interested investors. This places Staple Brite's stock in play because the potential buyers are interested in buying the stock at the current price to profit down the line.

Stocks in play are volatile and move in value enough to ensure the possibility that a day trader can make a profit on either bullish or bearish stock price movements. Stocks have to have specific characteristics to make it on that list. Those qualities include being highly volatile, highly liquid, and having a large volume.

So, how do you locate such stocks? Don't worry! It's not hard. Most brokers provide a platform where you can identify stocks that are currently in play. Hint, hint! You might want to make that a criterion when searching for the right brokerage representation for you. You do not have to rely on this approach exclusively. There are other ways to find stocks in play. It can be done by searching and using websites that provide information. Using stock screening tools is a great option. Keeping abreast of the news on major networks like the BBC and CNN is the right choice. They regularly provide financial reports.

FLOAT AND MARKET CAPITALIZATION

Looking for stock in play is the only way that day traders can go about finding tradeable stock. The shares and loans shareholders have provided to the business is called equity value. The free-float methodology is a viable option for day traders. This method relies on calculating the market capitalization of a company of interest. It's done by dividing the company's equity value by the shares that it has readily available on the stock market. For instance, a company with 100,000 available shares of stock priced at $100 has a market capitalization of $10,000,000. This gives day traders a great scope of market price movement on stock. It's more accurate than the full market capitalization method, which accounts for all the company's shares on the market. Therefore, the free-float method excludes shares that are:

- Locked in by the company

- Held by the government

- Acquired through a foreign direct investment method (which means an investment made by an individual or firm into business interests in a different country)

- Held by promoters

Because of its accuracy, the free-float method is used by significant Indexes globally. This method shows the day trader a more accurate reflection of the stock's volatility and its potential to earn the day trader a profit. It should be noted that a smaller free-float is more volatile. Fewer trades move the price more drastically, limiting the number of shares available to be traded. On the other hand, a larger free-float is less volatile. More trades move the price drastically, making a higher number of shares available to be traded.

PRE-MARKET GAPPERS METHOD

Day traders can further expand on a smaller free-float niche but using the gapper method. This method uses stock scanning tools, and the criteria set is to look up gaps that are more than 4%. This needs to be done in preparation for the trading day. It is a method that I implement as part of a daily pre-market routine, and it has served me well over the years. Luckily, all the information is presented by your scanning tool, so not complicated processes are needed.

This method is fast and effective and allows me to develop a game plan even before the market opens.

INTRADAY SCANS IN REAL-TIME

Day traders should make further use of stock scanner tools to find the tradeable stock. This allows the trader to keep up with the ever-change stock market. Some of the criteria that should be used for intraday scans include:

- **Volume Breakouts**. Stocks that are trading at higher than usual volume indicate price volatility, which presents an excellent opportunity for day traders.

- **Price Breakouts**. Use your stock scanning tools to locate stock price movements moving above or below the norm for analysis.

- **Volume**-**Weighted Average Price Breakouts**. This is a benchmark that indicates the price a stock has traded throughout the day. This is based on price and volume activity. It is crucial to look for stocks that are above or below this average. This is calculated by adding the amount traded then dividing the answer by the number of stock shared traded. If the average price was 400 and the shares totaled 20, the volume-weighted average price would be 20.

CHAPTER SUMMARY

- Day traders do not just trade a company's stock because it shows excellent traits for investing in. Most company's stocks are relatively constant in nature and move very slow in either direction. They only shift in value in powerful ways. This allows traders to make big profits when the

133

company produces negative or positive trading actions, which only typically happens a couple of times per year.

- Day traders need to find tradeable stocks to make a profit. Trading stock in play is an excellent strategy for doing so. Stocks are in play when they belong to a company purchased by another entity like another company or individual. This makes the stock volatile and more likely to earn a day trader a profit.

- The free-float methodology is a viable option for day traders to determine the best stock for trading. This method relies on calculating the market capitalization of a company of interest. This is done by dividing the company's equity value by the shares that it has readily available on the stock market. This gives day traders a great scope of market price movement and, thus, the stock's volatility.

- Day traders can further expand on a located smaller free-float niche but using the gapper method. This method uses stocker scanning tools. The criteria set is to look up gaps that are more than 4% as a pre-market preparation routine.

- The use of stock scanning tools fitted with criteria like volume breakouts, price breakouts, and volume-weighted average price breakouts also help with locating outstanding stocks for day trading.

ADVANCED TACTICS

Grasping the Trading Strategies

CHAPTER 13: LIGHT THOSE CANDLESTICKS

As mentioned in earlier parts of this book, several types of charts can perform technical analysis of stocks when finding the best ones to trade. This chapter is dedicated to showing you how to read charts and graphs in the most advantageous way to make a profit. I will shine a light on candlestick graphs. They are one of the most popular and informative types of charts available to day traders.

HOW TO READ CHARTS AND GRAPHS

In the world of the trading line charts, bar and candlestick charts are some of the most informative and easily accessed types of tools. They allow traders to make determinations about stocks and their activity on the stock market. The line chart is the most basic type of chart, but it is the one that most newbie day traders start with, and there is a reason for this. This chart's simplicity allows the day trader to focus on the essential element that is focused on the closing price, which is a reference point that shows security performance over time of a stock over a determined period. There is no information about highs and lows or on the opening prices, only closing prices over a predetermined amount of time.

After the beginner day trader has mastered line charts, he or she will expand into bar charts. Bar charts are constructed of a series of vertical lines representing information over a particular amount of time. Bar charts display information about opening and closing prices the open price on the vertical bar's left side. In contrast, the close price is located on the horizontal line and the bar's right side.

The bar chart shows increases and decreases in stock prices via a color scheme. Suppose the available price represented by the left bar is lower than the right, which is the closing price. In that case, the bar will be shaded in blue, black, or green to represent a price increase. There's also a decrease in the stock price. This happens when the left dash representing the open price is lower than the right one representing the closing price. This decrease is indicated by the color red.

After a beginner day trader has mastered the line and bar chart, it'll be time to move on to the candlestick chart. It will become easier to understand after using trade tools. The candlestick chart is similar to the bar chart. Its vertical lines represent stock price change over a particular time. There is a difference in color representation over a matter of time.

13-1 Simple candlestick chart image

Before we delve into how to read a candlestick chart like a pro, let us take a moment to look into the history of candlestick charts. It's essential to know how they have helped shape the day trading world into today.

WHAT ARE CANDLESTICKS IN DAY TRADING?

The effectiveness of the candlestick chart relies on technical analysis to determine patterns in price movement. This price chart indicates technical analysis. It displays the high, low, opening, and closing prices of a stock over a specific amount of time. The candlestick chart dates back to the 17th century, when Japanese rice merchants used to track market prices. The candlestick chart became popularized in the USA in the 1900s.

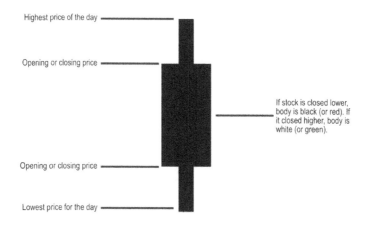

13-2 Close up image of a candlestick

The candlestick chart gets its name from the basic structure of the data representation, which resembles a candlestick. The body of the candlestick is color red or black if stock prices closed lower. In contrast, an increase in the closing price is really represented by a white for green body. The highest price of the day is represented at the top of the candlestick structure. In contrast, the lowest price of the day is represented at the bottom. The candlestick's shape can vary based on the interaction between that day's high low opening, and closing prices. The valuable nature of the data provided by the candlestick makes it not only useful in trading stock but also trading futures and foreign exchange. It's visually easy to read.

Candlestick charts come in two different types: bullish candlesticks and bearish candlesticks. Both of these candlesticks indicate price action and thus lead to a mass action due to the psychology they induce in traders. The typical pattern that generates mass excitement consists of two parts. The first part consists of a slow but increasing trend. Next, that trend picks up speed to gain a steep angle on the candlestick chart. The second part consists of a price reversal that is sharp in nature. For example, a stock price may have been $45, then slowly rose to $60 only to sharply decline to $44.

Traders use this price movement pattern to either identify a trend to capitalize on or notice a trend reversal to ride the train. Either way, day traders need to ride both upward and downward trends using technical analysis to make the best moves. *Technical analysis* is the analysis of patterns obtained from trading, particular patterns of price movement and volume.

No matter the direction of the trend, here are a few tips for having the best chance at making a profit:

- Do not make predictions. Wait for clear signs before making trades.

- Use confirmation tools to verify changes in market prices and price momentum changes, whether they are going up or down.

- Do not hold on to trading positions for too long. Being greedy will only risk the profits that you have already potentially made.

CANDLESTICKS TRENDS AND PATTERNS

The following are a few candlestick patterns that day traders use. The idea is not to search for these patterns but to get to a point where you can anticipate them. They are a useful analytical take on trading, but in no way effective without A LOT more back information.

These patterns are based on common movement trends where you intend to set your buy and sell. Which is fair. But, to get to a place where these trends or patterns become useful, there must be longitudinal examination, constant attention, or a program to understand them. All these trends are singular or multiple variations of up or down. Which up or down will it be? To notice the beginning of any of these patterns is an excellent place to be. This would give you the ability to gamble on which trends you'll likely see.

At the heart of it all, you will be able to make informed assumptions. You'd need to get to the level of seeing these trends before they happen. The more you practice, the better you get at finding and anticipating familiar patterns.

We'll go over some candlestick patterns here, but I also have a candlestick cheat sheet for you to familiarize yourself with them. You can find them here: bit.ly/NoobsCheatSheet.

Day trading can be like a full-time job, especially when you're first learning.

BULLISH CANDLESTICKS

These types of candlesticks are green or white on the chart. In this book, you'll see mostly white candlesticks to represent green ones. In a colorful candlestick chart, usually, you would see green. Don't get confused. Green and white mean the same thing. They indicate that the close price is higher than the open price. As a result, bullish candlesticks indicate buying pressure after or within the period that signals price movement reversal. There are common patterns that fall within that bullish candlestick pattern, and they include:

- **Hammer:** a green candlestick with a short body and a long low wick. This kind of bullish candlestick is highly recommended for use at support levels. It indicates that buying pressure is driving the price of the stock up.

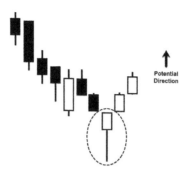

13-3 Image of hammer candlestick pattern.

- **Inverted hammer:** a green candlestick with a short body and a long upper wick. This is also called the shooting star and is, in essence, a reverse hammer hence the name. It is recommended for use near resistance levels and indicates that the price will soon be driven by buyer demand.

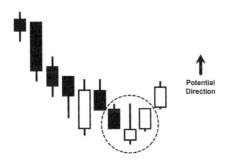

13-4 Image of inverted hammer candlestick pattern.

- **Bullish engulfing**: Consists of two candlesticks. The first candlestick is red and short and is dominated by the larger green candlestick.

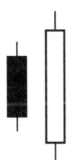

13-5 Image of Bullish engulfing candlestick pattern.

- **Piercing line**: This is also a two-candlestick pattern. Both the red and green candlesticks are long. A significant gap between the red closing and the green opening price indicates a significant buying pressure.

13-6 Image of Piercing Line candlestick pattern.

- **Morning star**: This signifies that things are looking up on the market after a downward trend. This is a three-candlestick pattern consisting of one short red candlestick and two long candlesticks, a red and green.

Potential
Direction

13-7 Image of morning star candlestick pattern.

- **Doji**: This candlestick pattern is excellent for use at both the support and resistance level. This is a complicated four-candlestick pattern that indicated a push and pulled between buyers in the market.

13-8 Image of doji candlestick pattern.

You must know how to read these types of charts as a day trader because, along with moving averages, they help you realize patterns that are spaced off just minutes apart. That is a tremendous asset for a day trader who buys and sells stocks and other securities several times in one day. A day trader can identify bullish trends on candlestick charts by noticing when the stock of interest forms higher highs and vice versa with the lows. Highs are known as peaks, and lows are known as valleys. All this picture is missing is a beautiful sunset, and I would be a happy man.

BEARISH CANDLESTICKS

Bearish candlesticks are typically indicated by the color red or black on charts. In this book, you'll mostly see the black candlesticks. Don't get confused by the colors. Red and black candlesticks are the same thing when you see them. With bearish candlesticks, the close price is lower than the open price. This is an indication that the price of the stock or other security is going down. Typically, option buyers use short and put strategies to ride the downward trend in price in such a market. A put strategy is a technique that can be used by traders or investors to generate income or purchase stocks at a reduced price. As an illustration, a trader may use a put option on stock with a strike price of $50. They'd have an expectation that it will be worth $45 in 6 months, thus selling the stock at a higher price to make a profit. The strike price

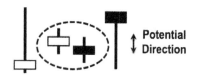

is when the put option holder can sell the underlying security. A day trader needs to be familiar with bearish candlesticks. They indicate when selling pressure is setting in on the market because the stock price or the security is going down.

For your information, when a trader sells a security first with the intention of repurchasing it or covering it later at a lower price, a short position is made. When the trader believes that the price of that security is likely to decrease in the near future, the trader will decide to short a security. Short covering refers to buying back the shares you borrowed to short.

I strongly advise against shorting as a beginner. There can be no limit to what you can lose, especially when you don't know the market well.

Other than the typical bearish candlestick, day traders need to be familiar with bearish reversal candlestick. It indicates that the stock's price shows an upward trend before it reverses its current downward trend. A sign that this is the future for the stock is found at critical support levels. The level buyers tend to purchase or enter a stock.

Types of bearish candlestick patterns include:

- **Hanging man**: This is equivalent to the hammer, but the shape of the candlestick is inverted.

13-9 Image of hanging man candlestick pattern.

- **Shooting star**: This is equivalent to the inverted hammer, but the candlestick's shape is inverted.

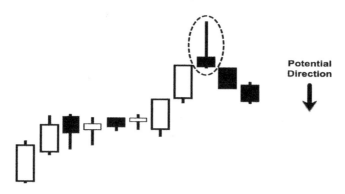

13-10 Image of shooting star candlestick pattern.

- **Bearish engulfing**: This type of bearish candlestick pattern indicated an impending downward trend in the market with two candlesticks. The first candlestick is green with a

150

short body, followed by the second candlestick, red with a long body.

13-11 Image of bearish engulfing candlestick pattern.

- **Evening star**: This is a three-candlestick pattern. It is the reverse of a bullish morning star and is indicative of a downward trend after an uptrend. This candlestick pattern consists of a short green candlestick sandwiched between a longer red and green candlestick.

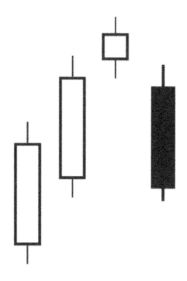

13-12 Image of evening star candlestick pattern.

INDECISION CANDLESTICKS

Sometimes, the market and the candlestick chart do not give hints about the direction price movement is heading. It is not bullish or bearish. This means that neither buyers nor sellers are being favored at a particular time.

This begs the question of what you should do if you're faced with an indecisive candlestick chart. The short answer is that it is usually better to stay on the sideline in such situations. Do not force yourself to make trades just because you feel that you should. There will be times such as these where the market does not swing either way. Protect your money in such a time instead of shooting shots in the dark. I run several small businesses on the side and focus my attention on them when I find the market is dominated by indecisive candlesticks. You should consider other side hustles as well. As the saying goes, never put all your eggs in one basket.

Here's an extra gift, Flashcards that can help you work to memorize candle stick patterns. You can cut them out and practice them as you please. Visit the following link and download them free now! bit.ly/CandlesticksForNoobs.

CHAPTER SUMMARY

- Charts and graphs are the backbones of the day trading career, and three of the most popular charts and graphs used by all day traders are the line chart, bar chart, and candlestick chart.

- The candlestick chart is the most basic type of chart that most beginners use at the start of their careers. This inclination is because of the chart's simplicity. The line chart displays closing prices over a specific amount of time using plot points of data.

- After a beginner has mastered the line chart, they will graduate to the bar chart. This type of chat displays information about the open and closing prices of stock with vertical lines. Bar charts show information about opening and closing prices; the open price is on the left side of the vertical bar. In contrast, the close price is located on the horizontal line and is on the bar's right side. The bar chart shows increases and decreases in stock prices via a color scheme. Blue, black, or green represents a price increase. A decrease is indicated by the color red.

- After a beginner day trader has mastered the line and bar chart, it is time to move on to the candlestick chart. The candlestick chart has many similarities to the bar chart. Still, a few fundamental differences, such as color representation, make it a more informative tool. The candlestick structure from which the candlestick chart gets its name is colored black or red to show increases in stock prices or green or white to show decreases in stock prices. The candlestick structure's top shows the highest of the day, while the handle stick structure's bottom represents the day's lowest price.

- Candlestick charts come in two different types: bullish candlesticks and bearish candlesticks. Both of these candlesticks indicate price action and thus lead to a mass action due to the psychology they induce in traders.

- Bullish candlesticks are green or white on the chart. They indicate that the close price is higher than the open price and that the stock price is going up. A few bullish candlestick patterns include the hammer, the inverted hammer, and the morning star.

- Bearish candlesticks are typically indicated by the color red or black on charts. With bearish candlesticks, the close price is lower than the open price. This is an indication that the price of the stock or other security is going down. A few types of bearish candlestick patterns include hanging man, shooting star, and bearish engulfing.

CHAPTER 14: TIME FOR SOME STRATEGIES

Knowing the right industries, companies, and stocks to invest in will do you no good if you have weak strategies to back them. This chapter discusses the strategies that all day traders should know if you want the most successful career possible.

POSITION SIZING AND TRADE MANAGEMENT

The first strategy is determining the proper position size of day trading stock. Position size refers to several shares that a day trader takes on when making a trade. Trading too little or too much can put a day trader at a disadvantage. The position size is the conditions that determine how much capital you allocate to a given trade. Taking a position size that is too big is much more of a risk than taking a position size that is too small. The risk of position size is two-fold. These two parts include the risk of the trade itself and its risk on the day trader's account.

Therefore, to ensure that the risk is minimized on both parts, the day trader needs to be strategic with position size. The day trader can mitigate this risk in three ways. First, they need to set their trading account with a dollar percentage risk limit for each trade. A strategic move is to have less than a 1% risk on the trading account. For example, the 1% risk on a $250,000 account is $2500.

Once the account has been set up to minimize risks, the day trader needs to focus on reducing risk on the particular trade being made. An excellent strategy for doing so is called the cents at risk strategy. This uses a stop-loss order so that trade is exited once a certain amount of money is lost. For instance, it's like automatically backing out of a $1000 order if $100 is lost. This stop-loss order enforces the limit that a day trader has placed on the trader account.

Lastly, the day trader needs to determine his or her position size by using the following formula:

Best Position Size = Money at Risk / Cents at Risk.

Therefore, if there's a 1% risk of the trading account, which has $35,000, the day trader can risk up to $350. This is the money at risk. Let's say the day trader is considering a stock that can be purchased for $50.00. They place a stop-loss limit in this at $49.87, which places a $0.13 at risk. This is the cents at risk value.

To arrive at the best position size, the formula above is used. This will gain a value of $2693.31. This will then be rounded to the nearest full hundred because most stocks are sold by 100 shares. Therefore, in this example, the best position size would be $2600.00.

SUPPORTS/ RESISTANCES

Support and resistance levels arise as day traders analyze chart patterns. Think of support and resistance levels as barriers that prevent price movement from being pushed too far in one direction. Support arises during downtrends due to a concentration of demand for the stock. Resistance is on the flip side of the coin and arises due to uptrends because there is a supply concentration. Both support and resistance levels can be identified on price charts using moving average dreams and the trend lines.

Day traders need to acknowledge support and resistance levels. This allows them to know what position to take when entering a trade. And when to buy and sell to exit. The primary method is to take a long position or buy where support levels are supported and do the opposite where resistance levels are supported. To manage risks using this strategy, place a stop-loss limit below support levels or a stop-loss limit above resistance levels when trading.

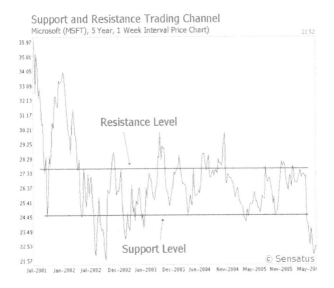

14-1 Image of support and resistance levels.

THE ABCD

This strategy is a great one for determining when and at what stage to enter and exit a day trade. It provides consistent data on how the market is moving. The ABCD pattern looks like a lightning bolt on a price chart and consists of 3 consecutive price movements. This pattern helps day traders identify trading opportunities on the market and highlight the risks compared to the potential profit of making a trade.

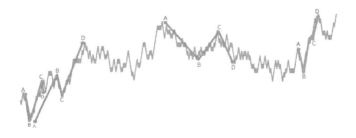

14-2 Image of a live example of ABCD patterns.

ABCD patterns come in both bearish and bullish varieties. Bearish ABCD patterns signal that a day trader should take a short position or sell. Bullish ABCD patterns signal that a day trader should take a long position or take the opportunity to buy stock.

Whether the ABCD pattern is bearish or bullish, the A B and C D lines are called legs, while the B C line is called a correction. The rules of the ABCD pattern are the same whether or not the pattern is bearish or bullish. The only differing factor is the direction of the price movement of the stock. A bearish ABCD pattern follows an uptrend that has the potential for bearish investment at the reversal of the down levels. On the other hand, bullish ABCD patterns follow a downtrend that signals the potential for the reversal of the upside. It's vital to note that the day trader must only trade after the price movement reaches point D. If not, the day trader would have done all that analyzing for nothing. That would be quite the bummer!

14-3 Image of bearish ABCD pattern

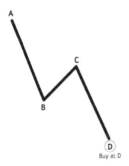

14-4 Image of bullish ABCD pattern

OPENING RANGE BREAKOUTS

The opening range describes the low and high prices of a given time during the stock market's operating hours.

161

Once the market opens, at 9:30 AM EST, it's typically the most significant price movements of the day, which lasts for an hour. This time frame is the most important and volatile. The initial 15 to 30 trading minutes set the pace for the trading day, where you're examining and observing the market. Hence, on a candlestick chart, the first 30 minutes of trading within the lows and highs is called the opening range.

The first thing that needs to be done when working with this strategy is identifying high and low prices. Next, identify the highs and lows of previous periods for comparisons.

Using this information, day traders can put themselves in a prime position for taking advantage of the opening hour of the stock market. This time is typically highly volatile, with significant trading volume. A day trader can use the opening range to determine entry positions based on its size. This size can be provided from the high and low of the candlesticks created from the last trading session of the previous day. The difference between the high and low of the current day's candlestick price and the high and low of the last session of the previous day's candlestick gives a measure of the size of the opening range.

One of the most critical parts of using the opening range strategy is finding its breakout. Breakout determines price direction. Suppose the price breaks out of the opening range. In that case, there is a considerable probability that the price movement will continue in that same direction. Always manage the risks of this strategy with stop-loss orders.

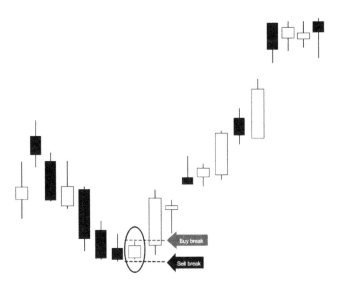

14-5 Image of opening range price breakout.

BULL FLAG MOMENTUM

This day trading strategy relies on using patterns on the candlestick chart to determine trends that are likely to be profitable. The bull flag momentum shows a strong upward trend in stock price movement and looks like a flag on a pole, hence the name. Because the price movement is up, the trend is described as bullish.

A bull flag pattern has the following qualities:

- Substantial upward relative volume to form the pole.

- Consolidation near the top of the pole indicates lighter volume and, thus, the flag's formation.

- Breakouts on relatively high volume for the continuation of the upward trend.

14-6 Image of bull flag chart pattern.

Using this strategy is simple and more difficulty comes from locating the pattern. The use of stock scanner tools will allow this location, though. The best strategy is to buy when the stock prices breakout above the point of a consolidation. A stop order should be placed below the point of a consolidation. Consolidation refers to when a stock or security trades within a range. The stock doesn't move much in its price trend.

The bull flag momentum strategy contrasts with the bear flag strategy. Bear flag momentum shows a strong downward trend in the stock price movement, described as bearish. This pattern's best strategy is to sell when the stock prices break out below a consolidation point. A stop order should be placed above the point of a consolidation.

14-7 Image of bear flag chart pattern.

REVERSAL TRADING

This type of day trading strategy relies on entering a position near a support level so that the trader can potentially profit on the reversal of current market trends. Reversals can be used in both bullish and bearish market conditions. The reversal should be practiced on the downside when the trend was bullish and vice versa in bearish conditions. Signs of a reversal are the accumulation of volume and price. These are generally small in nature to start and are called consolidations of pullbacks. Consolidations and reversals can be indistinguishable to the untrained eye. Still, where consolidations end, reversals continue and form a new trend in the opposite direction.

When the upward trend begins to terminate, price and volume begin to decline. This forces a downward break in price that leads to a reversal. Think of this method as expertly catching a knife that was thrown into the air when it descends. That would be rather kickass, wouldn't it? And might I add, thoroughly impressive.

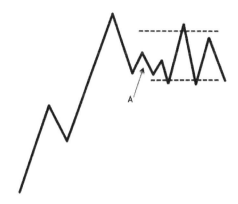

14-8 Image of trend termination.

MOVING AVERAGE TREND TRADING

This day trading strategy makes use of a technical analysis tool. This creates average stock prices update continuously for specific periods like 20 minutes or any other period that a day trader chooses as the criteria. This trading strategy is beneficial because it can be tailored to display stock price averages. It also allows day traders to tune out the noise to get specific information about price fluctuations. This benefits them in that day's interval. Day trading is not for the faint of heart because of how quickly the market can shift. Therefore, you need to access the information you need when you need it instead of continually wading through tons of numbers.

Using the moving average strategy allows you to do just that.

This trading strategy also allows the traders that identified support and resistance levels in addition to price direction. Uptrends act like support, while downtrends act as resistance.

There are different types of moving average strategies. One of the most commonly used is called a simple moving average. It displays a basic price movement over a specific period. For instance, a 20-period simple moving average will show the 20 previous closing prices divided by the number of periods, 20, to determine the simple moving average's current value. This will be joined to form a simple line on a price chart like the candlestick chart. Periods of 50, 100, and 200 are also commonly used.

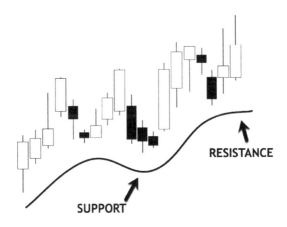

14-9 Image of moving average pattern.

VWAP TRADING

VWAP stands for the volume-weighted average price, while MVWAP stands for moving volume-weighted average price. Both of these prices are used in short-term trading to ensure that day traders get the best price deals. While MVWAP can also be used by longer-term traders, VWAP provides the best data for day traders. It only provides information for 1-day periods because it is calculated on an intraday period.

Both provide a great view of the volume provided at an average price and provide useful stock scanning tools. Generally, the best-accepted strategy for VWAP is to sell if the stock price is above VWAP and buy the stock if the price is below VWAP.

14-10 VWAP vs. MVWAP.

RED-TO-GREEN TRADING

This day trading strategy relies on using the previous day's close price to determine the entry position day traders should make. If the close price is below the previous day's close price, this indicates "red." If the reverse is correct and the stock's close price is above the previous day's close price, this is considered "green." The previous close price indicates support and resistance levels.

Suppose a stock price moves from red to green. In that case, this is considered a significant momentum shift because the stock price is elevated from below the previous close price to above the previous close price. This makes the stock more volatile and makes it a worthy risk for gaining rewards from day trading. Green is indicative of a bullish condition, and many day traders use this as an opportunity to take a long position. Red is not a lost cause, though. It indicated bearish conditions. You can only use this as an opportunity to take a short position to trade stock.

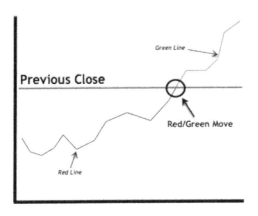

14-11 Image of red-to-green trading pattern.

HOW TO TRADE WITH TRAILING STOPS

This strategy is based on limiting day trader losses. One of the best exit strategies is placing a stop-loss order. If stock prices go below a certain level, then the day trading position will automatically be closed. Day traders can

171

take this risk management up another level by coupling stop-loss orders with trailing stops.

Trailing stops are trade orders that work where stop-loss orders are not fixed to a one-dollar amount. Instead, trailing stops work best when the day trade limit is a certain percentage or dollar amounts below the stock market price.

Trailing stop work by moving along increasing stock prices. When this increase stops, a new stop-loss price is created due to the trailing order being dragged with the stock price. This reduces the day trader's risk while still locking in as much profit as possible with the trade as the stock price rises to higher values.

BASING TRADE ON THE TIME OF DAY

As noted above, the best trading time is the opening hour of the stock market. The stock market opens at 9:30 AM EST time. Therefore, the most volatile and high-volume time is between 9:30 AM and 10:30 AM EST. You need to be on the ball to be active on the stock market no matter where in the world you live or what time you are operating with. Do what you need to do to develop a pre-market routine to keep your mind sharp at that time.

Other times of the day can be profitable as well. Thus, you need to develop rituals that will reveal that to you in your particular instance. A great way to do this is to review your performance at the end of your trading day.

The stock market closes at 4:00 PM EST. When this happens, note the number of trades that you made at what times, the number of winning and losing trades made, the active number of hours that you trade, and your net profit or loss for the day.

DISCOVERING YOUR OWN STRATEGY

Whew! That was quite a considerable number of details packed in this chapter. But knowledge is empowerment no matter the ballgame, and that holds true for day trading. All the strategies outlined above are great for raking in profits when implemented correctly. Still, no amount of knowledge will benefit you until you get in the game and get your feet wet.

As a day trader, you will learn to find what works best for you through experimentation. You can create your own strategies by assessing charts, being curious and interested, and having a willingness to continually learn. Don't approach creating your own strategies with apprehension. You'll only give yourself a massive headache. I can personally attest to this in my early years of day trading. Creating personalized day trading strategies can be a fun, creative, and easy process once you approach it with an open mind.

The steps to creating a day strategy include:

- Assess the type of day trader that you are.

- Assess your time zone and how this affects the time that you work on the stock market.

- Assess the times of securities that you will trade-in.

- Look at historical data to see what has worked for others in the past.

- Create trading rules for yourself, such as entry and exit points.

- Test other strategies to see how well they incorporate with your overall plan.

- Develop contingency plans if things do not work out as planned.

CHAPTER SUMMARY

- Some of the best day trading strategies include position sizing, which is several shares that a day trader takes on when making a trade. Position sizing lowers the risk of day trading stock. This is done by putting a limit on a day trader's account and a stop-loss limit of trades to arrive at the best position size that should be handled with each trade.

- The next strategy uses the ABCD pattern, which looks like a lightning bolt on a price chart and consists of 3 consecutive price movements. This pattern helps day traders identify trading opportunities on the market and highlight the risks compared to the potential profit of making a trade. This pattern comes in both bearish and bullish varieties.

Another strategy called the bull flag momentum relies on using patterns on the candlestick chart to determine trends that are likely to be profitable. The bull flag momentum shows a strong upward (bullish) trend in stock price movement and looks like a flag on a pole, hence the name.

- High volume allows day traders to buy when the stock prices breakout above the point of a consolidation. The bear flag pattern is the direct opposite of the bull flag pattern.

- The reversal trading strategy relies on entering a position near a support level so that the trader can potentially profit from the reversal of current market trends. Reversal trading can be used in both bullish and bearish market conditions.

- The moving average day trading strategy makes use of a technical analysis tool. It creates average stock prices updated continuously for specific periods like 20 minutes or any other period that a day trader chooses as the criteria. This trading strategy is beneficial. It can be tailored to display stock price averages at any time frame and provide a clear view of the price movement's direction.

- Support and resistance levels are barriers that prevent price movement from being pushed too far in one direction. Support arises during downtrends due to a concentration of demand for the stock. Resistance is on the flip side of the coin and arises due to uptrends because there is a supply concentration. Day traders can use this knowledge to take a long position or buy where support levels are supported. They can also do the opposite where resistance levels are supported.

- VWAP stands for a volume-weighted average price. Day traders can use this value 1-day period worth of information to determine the volume at average prices. This allows for the development of strategies of when to buy and sell the stock.

- The red-to-green day trading strategy relies on using the previous day's close price to determine the entry position that a day trader should make. If the close price of a stock is below the previous day's close price, this indicates "red." If the reverse is correct and the stock's close price is above the previous day's close price, this is considered "green." Red to green indicates price volatility and sets up prime conditions for day traders to profit.

- The opening range describes the low and high prices of a given period, like 30 and 60 minute periods during the stock market's operating hours. Like I said, the first thing that needs to be done when working with this strategy is identifying high and low prices. Next, identify the highs and lows of previous periods for comparisons. These are needed to determine the price direction for making trades.

- The use of trailing stop works to limit losses while ensuring that day traders make maximum profits on trades. Trailing stops are trade orders that work where stop-loss orders are not fixed to a one-dollar amount. Instead, trailing stops work best when the day trade limit is a certain percentage or dollar amounts below the stock market price.

- Another simple day trading strategy is to ensure that you are on the ball for the first hour of trading. This is 9:30 AM to 10:30 EM EST time because of the high volatility and volume found. Also, develop strategies to find out the best trading times for you personally.

- You can also create your own trading strategies with a little creativity and a willingness to learn and experiment.

Conclusion

You can live a life that is free of money, stress, and headache. You just have to have the courage to go out on a limb and embrace a challenge.

Day trading is a proven solution that has given thousands of people the tools they need to be financially free. So, they can pursue the things that make them happy and bring them enjoyment. They choose how they spend their time and are not locked to a particular location or job. You can live such a reality too!

We have discussed several topics in this book ranging from what day trading is to how you can develop the psychology that will make you as successful as possible. Despite the compact nature, we have covered a comprehensive range of topics that will give you a good head start if you have decided (and I hope you have) that you have what it takes to make this field profitable for you.

At the start of this book, I promised to give you a realistic view of what it means to become a day trader. No career is all sunshine and rainbows, but day trading has the potential to gain you more than many other careers out there. Also, despite the amount of time you have to put in the beginning to typically see a profit, this is a relatively small amount of time for the magnitude by which you can benefit. Since I began my career, I have gained a friendship and acquaintanceship with many other day traders. They come from different walks of life and have different backgrounds from many different countries. They all have different goals and dreams. They all have small quirks and different approaches to daily routines. I know a day trader who only makes trades while listening to rock music in the background and another who has to do yoga before she starts her trading day. Yet still, they all benefit from day trading. That is why I am confident that you can also join this elite membership of people.

I invite you to join our community on Facebook. You can find it here bit.ly/NoobsTradingFacebook. let's all live to our potential together.

FINAL THOUGHTS

You can do this!

This book has shown that you do not have to be the brightest, smartest, or most talented to reap success. You only have to be passionate, excited and persistent in your effort to learn. Do not stop your day trading journey here. Read more, watch videos, and listen to podcasts. Gain mentorship. Put in the work and time. Experiment and practice until you find the right strategies that work for you personally. Resilience wins over talent and smarts every time. Resilience is what separates the winners from the losers. You are a winner! Embrace the fact and act like it! You may stumble and fall at times, but you will learn that getting dirty does not faze you. Not when this day trading game provides such a thrill… and grand profits. Watching your bank account grow is quite the motivator, I have found!

Thank you for purchasing this book, and good luck!

I ask you, humbly, to help

Congratulations for reading until the end.

Reviews help me create more books and improve others.

Please visit www.amazon.com to leave a review right now.

I thank you again from the bottom of my heart.

Many purchases are inspired by reviews, but only 8% of readers ever leave a review.

YOUR FREE GIFT

Thanks again for buying my book!

To show my appreciation, I would like to invite you to the For Noobs Book Club and send you a FREE BONUS BOOK: ***Stock Investing for Noobs - The Easiest Step-by-Step Investment Guide with Zero-Knowledge Prerequisite***

The perfect starting place to better understand stock investments in a simple and easy to understand language.

The book will cover:

- **"Finding the Right Industries to Invest In"** (finding industries that interest you, but also those that will be able to sail through economic storms).

- **"The Important Rules of Investing"** (approved tips to help you make the best use of your money).

- **"How to Value Stocks"** (Calculated predictions of how well a stock will do in the long and short term).

- **"Growth Investing Strategies"** (growth investing strategy focuses on businesses that have excellent growth value).

- And Much More!

To get your FREE copy of this book, visit the link below and sign up now:

>>>bit.ly/noobinvesting<<<

INDEX

REFERENCES

1. "Day Trading for a Living - The Good and Not So Good Things to Consider." 2018. Vantage Point Trading. July 10, 2018. https://vantagepointtrading.com/day-trading-living-good-not-good-things-consider/.

2. "Margin Rules for Day Trading." n.d. Accessed June 27, 2020. https://www.sec.gov/investor/alerts/daytrading.pdf.

3. comit. 2018. "Blueprint for Forex Day Trading with $1,000 (or Less)." Vantage Point Trading. April 28, 2018. https://vantagepointtrading.com/blueprint-forex-day-trading-1000-less/.

4. "How Much Money Do I Need to Become a Day Trader." 2018. Vantage Point Trading. February 14, 2018. https://vantagepointtrading.com/how-much-capital-do-i-need-to-start-day-trading-stocks/.

5. "Long and Short Positions - An Overview and Examples of Long/Short." n.d. Corporate Finance Institute. https://corporatefinanceinstitute.com/resources/knowledge/trading-investing/long-and-short-positions/.

6. "Why Day Traders Should Stick to the 1 Percent Rule (And How to Do It)." 2019. My Trading Skills. December 13, 2019. https://www.mytradingskills.com/one-percent-rule.

7. "Types of Orders | Investor.Gov." n.d. Www.Investor.Gov. Accessed June 27, 2020. https://www.investor.gov/introduction-investing/investing-basics/how-stock-markets-work/types-orders.

8. "Download Limit Exceeded." n.d. Citeseerx.Ist.Psu.Edu. Accessed June 27, 2020. http://citeseerx.ist.psu.edu/viewdoc/download?doi=10.1.1.418.2508&rep=rep1&type=pdf.

9. "Fidelity Learning Center: Technical Analysis Indicator Guide." n.d. Www.Fidelity.Com. Accessed June 27, 2020. https://www.fidelity.com/learning-center/trading-investing/technical-analysis/technical-indicator-guide/overview.

10. "Trade Order - Definition, Types, and Practical Examples." n.d. Corporate Finance Institute. https://corporatefinanceinstitute.com/resources/knowledge/trading-investing/trade-order/

11. "How To Pick A Forex Broker That Is Right For You". 2020. Vantage Point Trading. https://vantagepointtrading.com/pick-forex-broker-right/.

12. Team, Trading, and Maria Palma. 2020. "How To Use Stock Scanners: A Beginner's Guide - Stockstotrade.Com". Stockstotrade.Com. https://stockstotrade.com/how-to-use-stock-scanners/.

13. "Top Stock Screeners For Day Trading, Swing Trading, And Investing". 2020. Vantage Point Trading. https://vantagepointtrading.com/top-stock-screeners-for-day-trading-swing-trading-and-investing/.

14. "How To Read Trading Charts ▷ A Must-Read Guide | Friedberg Direct". 2020. Avatrade. https://www.avatrade.ca/education/trading-for-beginners/how-to-read-a-trading-chart.

15. "The "Boom And Bust" Pattern – Reading Mass Psychology From Your Charts -". 2020. Tradeciety Online Trading. https://www.tradeciety.com/boom-and-bust-trading-pattern/.

16. "Financial Ratios - Complete List And Guide To All Financial Ratios". 2020. Corporate Finance Institute. https://corporatefinanceinstitute.com/resources/knowledge/finance/financial-ratios/.

17. "What Is Market Cap? - Fidelity". 2020. Fidelity.Com. https://www.fidelity.com/learning-center/trading-investing/fundamental-analysis/understanding-market-capitalization/

18. "Difference Between Full Market Capitalization And Free Float Market Capitalization". 2020. https://Www.Goodreturns.In/. https://www.goodreturns.in/classroom/2015/11/difference-between-full-market-capitalization-free-float-market-capitalization-410197.html.

19. "A Simple Day Trading Strategy For Beginners: Gap And Go!". 2020. Warrior Trading. https://www.warriortrading.com/gap-go/.

20. "Volume Weighted Average Price (VWAP) Definition". 2020. Investopedia. https://www.investopedia.com/terms/v/vwap/.

21. "What Is Investment Position Sizing?". 2020. Investopedia. https://www.investopedia.com/terms/p/positions izing/.

22. "ABCD Pattern | FOREX.Com". 2020. Forex.Com. https://www.forex.com/en-ca/education/education-themes/technical-analysis/abcd-pattern/.

23. "Reversal Day Trading Strategies For Beginners | Warrior Trading". 2020. Warrior Trading. https://www.warriortrading.com/reversal-trading-strategy/.

24. Team, Trading. 2020. "5 Tips To Efficiently Building A Daily Watchlist - Stockstotrade.Com". Stockstotrade.Com. https://stockstotrade.com/building-a-watchlist/.

25. "How Long It Takes to Become a Successful Trader." 2018. Vantage Point Trading. May 7, 2018. https://vantagepointtrading.com/how-long-does-it-take-become-a-successful-trader-the-thorough-answer/

IMAGE SOURCES

10-1
https://commons.wikimedia.org/wiki/File:ESignal_versi
on_11_2_screenshot.png

10-2
https://commons.wikimedia.org/wiki/File:ESignal_versi
on_11_2_screenshot.png

13-1
https://commons.wikimedia.org/wiki/File:Candlestick_
Chart_in_MetaTrader_5.png

14-1
https://en.wikipedia.org/wiki/File:MicrosoftSupportRes
istanceTradingChannelChart.JPG

Made in the USA
Middletown, DE
28 September 2021